_For_

_____

_From_

_____

_Date_

_____

# Wonderful Names

## of our

# Wonderful Lord

CHARLES HURLBURT AND T.C. HORTON

BARBOUR
PUBLISHING

Published by Barbour Publishing, Inc., P.O. Box 719, Uhrichsville, Ohio 44683
www.barbourbooks.com

*Our mission is to publish and distribute inspirational products offering exceptional value and biblical encouragement to the masses.*

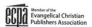
Member of the
Evangelical Christian
Publishers Association

Printed in China.

# Day 1

## *The Seed of the Woman*

*And I will put enmity between thee and the woman,
and between thy seed and her seed.*

GENESIS 3:15

"Because He stooped so low God hath exalted Him very high"
(Philippians 2:9, Arthur Way's Translation). From this first great act
and fact in His revelation to that last greater act when He died for our
sins on Calvary, and up until the time when God exalted Him very
high to sit at His own right hand in the heavens, our Savior's example
was one of profound humility. He came from the bosom of the Father
to become the "Seed of the Woman." He turned from "the words
which I have spoken to you, the same shall judge you," to be in His
innocence judged of sinful men and crucified.

*Oh, Lord who did humble Yourself to be born of a woman, who did
bear our sins in Your own body on the tree, we bow on our faces
before You and worship and adore. Amen.*

.................................................................................................

.................................................................................................

.................................................................................................

.................................................................................................

# Day 2

## *The Angel of the Lord*

*And the angel of the LORD called unto
Abraham out of heaven the second time.*
**GENESIS 22:15**

The Angel (or Messenger) of the Lord was Himself God's message
to us.

*Oh Lord, who Yourself bring Your own Message to heal our deepest
grief—You are our sin offering. We praise You for the glory which
You give in our pain by Your own radiant presence and worship
You, oh Angel of the Lord. Amen.*

........................................................................................................................

........................................................................................................................

........................................................................................................................

........................................................................................................................

# Day 3

## *Shiloh (Peacemaker)*

*The sceptre shall not depart from Judah, nor a
lawgiver from between his feet, until Shiloh come;
and unto him shall the gathering of the people be.*
GENESIS 49:10

Israel must walk in darkness under law until the years may seem an
eternity, but "Shiloh" comes at last, and with Him, peace. Has Shiloh
come to you? And has the peace which surpasses understanding,
the peace *He* made, entered into your soul? For Shiloh came and
conquered every foe that could harass you and stands today offering
the peace He made "which passeth all understanding." Have you
received it? Has Shiloh come in vain for you? Begin today and "in
every thing by prayer and supplication with thanksgiving let your
requests be made known unto God," and Shiloh's peace "shall keep
your hearts" (Philippians 4:6–7).

.......................................................................................................................................

.......................................................................................................................................

.......................................................................................................................................

.......................................................................................................................................

# Day 4

## The Stone of Israel

*But his bow abode in strength, and the arms of his hands were made strong by the hands of the mighty God of Jacob; (from thence is the shepherd, the stone of Israel).*

GENESIS 49:24

Oh Stone of Israel, chief Cornerstone, rejected by the builders, Stone of Stumbling, Rock of Offense, Foundation Stone, on which alone we build anything that will stand, make me a polished, living stone, built in with other stones, perhaps a pillar to go out no more, but always a part of Your temple, for Your own indwelling. Three times Holy Lord, self-offered for my peace: through death that I might live, through fire that I might become indestructible, consumed that I might feed on You in holiest communion—enlighten me today till I perceive Your peace that surpasses understanding. Amen.

......................................................................................................

......................................................................................................

......................................................................................................

......................................................................................................

# Day 5

## Manna

*And the house of Israel called the name thereof Manna.*
EXODUS 16:31

There is an art, not known to all who travel, by which a wearied and exhausted life may gather—in a way which seems to those who do not understand almost miraculous—new strength, new vigor, new physical power for an onward march. So does the Master feed the souls of His children a spiritual "Manna" as real and more wonderful than that strange, mysterious food with which He fed the House of Israel. To "feed upon the Lord" may sound like empty mysticism but may be a fact to every trusting soul. For to us are given "exceeding great and precious promises: that by these ye might be partakers of the divine nature" (2 Peter 1:4).

.......................................................................................................................

.......................................................................................................................

.......................................................................................................................

.......................................................................................................................

# Day 6

## The Meat (Meal) Offering

*And when any will offer a meat offering unto the LORD,
his offering shall be of fine flour; and he shall pour oil upon it,
and put frankincense thereon.*

LEVITICUS 2:4

Perfect communion with our God as shown in the "Meat Offering"
was in many senses the highest pattern which our Savior set for men.
Will we not make it the foremost plan of every day to have a time
when we enter into such worship with Him that we may truly say,
"There is nothing between You and me, dear Lord," and then carry
the sweetness of that deep communion unmarred and uninterrupted
through all the hours.

*Most Holy Meal Offering, El Elyon, as You did pour on the fine
meal of Your perfect life the Holy Oil of Your most Holy Spirit, and
the frankincense of Your perfect adoration, and offer all for me, so I,
accepting Yours which only hallows mine, pour out my soul, my blood-
cleansed soul, in worship. Holy! Holy! Holy! is the Lord. Amen.*

...........................................................................................................

...........................................................................................................

...........................................................................................................

...........................................................................................................

# Day 7

## The Peace Offering

*And if his oblation be a sacrifice of peace offering. . .
he shall offer it without blemish before the LORD.*

LEVITICUS 3:4

Is there any point of dispute between the Lord and you? One little
thing which you have not surrendered? He is right. He cannot change.
It is *your* heart which must surrender. Then you can receive the peace
that surpasses knowledge. He has made the offering which atones for
all your past, but you must yield your will to Him. Will it be now?

..............................................................................................................................

..............................................................................................................................

..............................................................................................................................

..............................................................................................................................

# Day 8

## *A Star*

*I shall see him, but not now: I shall behold him,*
*but not nigh: there shall come a Star out of Jacob.*
NUMBERS 24:17

What could be more beautiful or more fitting than God calling our Lord "a Star"? Those who know Him best may say, "One day I will see him, but not now. I will behold him, but not from here." Far beyond our world of trouble and care and change, He shines with undimmed light, a radiant, guiding Star to all who will follow Him—a morning Star, promise of a better day.

.................................................................................................

.................................................................................................

.................................................................................................

.................................................................................................

# Day 9

*A Sceptre*

*A Sceptre shall rise out of Israel.*
NUMBERS 24:17

There is a view of Jesus which men are slow to see, but someday all the world will know that "a Sceptre" will rise out of Israel, and evil will be destroyed before His righteousness more swiftly than ice must melt before the glowing sun. It is in the very nature of things that sin must be consumed before His glorious holiness. Can it be anything other than the love of sin that blinds the eyes of men to His consuming righteousness?

*"Search me, O God, and know my heart: try me, and know my thoughts, and see if there be any wicked way in me, and lead me in the way everlasting" (Psalm 139:23–24). Amen.*

...................................................................................................

...................................................................................................

...................................................................................................

...................................................................................................

# Day 10

## The Captain of the Host of the Lord

*And he said, Nay;*
*but as captain of the host of the LORD am I now come.*
JOSHUA 5:14

The armies of Israel stand before the gateway to a promised land. No swords are drawn, no skill have they, but with them is an unseen force and, with that force, "The Captain of Jehovah's Host." Jericho and all the giants of the land submit, and for you, "behind the dim unknown stands God within the shadows, keeping watch over His own."

*Captain of the Hosts of God,*
*In the path where Thou hast trod,*
*Bows my soul in humble awe—*
*Take command. Thy word is law.*

*Cause me to possess the land,*
*Led by Thine Almighty hand.*
*Be my guide, defense, and power,*
*Lead me from this very hour. Amen.*

.................................................................................................

.................................................................................................

.................................................................................................

.................................................................................................

# Day 44

## *The Rock of My Salvation*

*The LORD liveth; and blessed be my rock;
and exalted be the God of the rock of my salvation.*
2 SAMUEL 22:47

No more grave a danger threatens the believer than that of forgetting he is redeemed—forgetting even in the joy of realized life what our salvation cost, and what is the rock foundation of our faith. To meet this need, our Savior pictures Himself not merely as the Rock of Ages and our Strong Rock of Refuge, but the *Rock of our Salvation.* In Him and on His merit and atoning grace, we were saved from among the lost. Let us celebrate in this precious name and never forget that He was "wounded for our transgressions" and "that he bore our sins in his own body on the tree."

.....................................................................................................................................

.....................................................................................................................................

.....................................................................................................................................

.....................................................................................................................................

# Day 12

## The Light of the Morning

*And he shall be as the light of the morning,*
*when the sun riseth, even a morning without clouds.*
2 Samuel 23:4

No single name or picture of our Lord could possibly reveal Him as the full supply of all our need. Our Lord is to His people not only "The Morning Star," but when the lights of night fade in dawning day, He becomes the "Light of the Morning." When all the earth has passed, when all of earth's visions fade and flee away, when the great glory of that morning of our eternal life in heaven shines on us, we will find that the One who lit all our earthly pilgrimage is still our source of life and guidance in heaven and will be to those for whom He has prepared a place the "Light of the Morning." "So shall we ever be with the Lord" (1 Thessalonians 4:17).

.............................................................................................

.............................................................................................

.............................................................................................

.............................................................................................

# Day 13

## The Tender Grass

*And he shall be. . .as the tender grass springing*
*out of the earth by clear shining after rain.*
2 SAMUEL 23:4

Sheep thrive best in pastures so low and short that other animals are
not able to eat there. The Good Shepherd leads His flock in pastures
where the "tender grass," springing up from the earth after the rain,
brings to them all-sufficient nourishment as they feed on Him. Oh,
you who are partakers of the divine nature, open now the Book of
books, and humbly kneeling, feed on Him who is the Living Word,
"The Tender Grass," which satisfies and builds up His hungry sheep.

.............................................................................................................

.............................................................................................................

.............................................................................................................

.............................................................................................................

# Day 14

## *The Daysman*

*Neither is there any daysman betwixt us,*
*that might lay his hand upon us both.*
JOB 9:33

When the day of reckoning comes, when by all justice I should hear the sentence which my sins deserve, when I stand before the Father stripped of all pretense and sham, then will I fear no evil, for my "Daysman," Mediator, Arbitrator, will stand and speak for me. Can I do less than bow down and worship Him, now, and throughout eternity?

........................................................................................................................

........................................................................................................................

........................................................................................................................

........................................................................................................................

# Day 15
## My Glory

*But thou, O Lord, art a shield for me;*
*my glory, and the lifter up of mine head.*
PSALM 3:3

That God is "glory"—or "excellence"—beyond our understanding, none can deny. But do our hearts look up to Him today in humble, earnest worship, and know the truth, and speak the truth—"You are My Glory"? Our *safety* lies in the fact that He possesses us. Our deepest, holiest *joy* comes only when we humbly say in the hour of secret worship, "You are mine."

*Oh Lord my Glory, be my shield this day. Amen.*

.......................................................................................................................................

.......................................................................................................................................

.......................................................................................................................................

.......................................................................................................................................

# Day 16

## The Lifter Up of Mine Head

*But thou, O LORD, art a shield for me; my glory,
and the lifter up of mine head.*

PSALM 3:3

*Oh, Thou who hast given
Thy glory to me,
Anoint my blind eyes
Till Thy glory I see.*

*Lift up my bowed head,
Be my shield and my light,
Till Thy radiant glory
Shall banish my night.*

.................................................................

.................................................................

.................................................................

.................................................................

# Day 17

## *Fortress*

*The LORD is my rock, and my fortress, and my deliverer;
my God, my strength, in whom I will trust; my buckler,
and the horn of my salvation, and my high tower.*

"A mighty fortress is my God," and no evil may reach the soul that
shelters there. There is no saint of God who may look back through all
the troubled years of any earthly pilgrimage and not say, if he speaks
truly, "I have been sustained by the power of God." Every failure
of our lives, and each defeat, has come when we have sought some
earthly fortress rather than our Lord.

*I am hiding, Lord, in You. Amen.*

.................................................................................................................................

.................................................................................................................................

.................................................................................................................................

.................................................................................................................................

# Day 18

## A Worm and No Man

*But I am a worm, and no man;*
*a reproach of men, and despised of the people.*
PSALM 22:6

Few harder experiences come to God's children than when those who should be friendly unjustly reproach us and say in the midst of our trials which are not the result of any sin in us, "Aha, aha," as though they themselves are righteous, when perhaps their sin has brought to us the pain—yet *He* has walked that way before us. He, too, was "A Reproach of Men"! Will not the servant walk there, too, and be like Him who in such suffering "openeth not His mouth" (Isaiah 53:7)?

*Lord Jesus, who bore scorn and reproach for me,*
*give me the grace of true humility. Amen.*

# Day 19
## *My Shepherd*

*The LORD is my shepherd; I shall not want.*
PSALM 23:1

To say "The Lord is my Shepherd" must carry with it in our understanding not merely grateful praise for the infinite grace and tenderness of the Great Shepherd who leads us by still waters and in green pastures, but confession of our own helplessness and need of a Shepherd's care. And a remembrance also of our lost, undone condition, until

*All through the mountains, thunder-riven,*
*And up from the rocky steep,*
*There arose a glad cry to the gates of heaven,*
*"Rejoice! I have found My sheep!"*

> *Lord Jesus, tender Shepherd, lead us forth*
> *this day in glad service for You. Amen.*

.......................................................................................................................................

.......................................................................................................................................

.......................................................................................................................................

.......................................................................................................................................

# Day 20

## *Restorer*

*He restoreth my soul:*
*he leadeth me in the paths of righteousness for his name's sake.*
PSALM 23:3

We wander from God and from the paths of righteousness—from following Him beside the still waters—till we lose the way, lose joy, lose the sound of His voice. Then the Master "restoreth {the only use of this form in the Old Testament} our soul"; "brings us back into his way," into the paths of righteousness.

*Oh gracious Restorer, bring back my wandering soul as*
*You would a straying sheep, and lead me on in the paths*
*of righteousness "for Your name's sake." Amen.*

.............................................................................................

.............................................................................................

.............................................................................................

.............................................................................................

# Day 24

## *The Strong and Mighty Lord*

*Who is this King of glory?*
*The LORD strong and mighty, the LORD mighty in battle.*
PSALM 24:8

Is your heart faint? Your strength nothing but utter weakness? Behold your Lord—Jehovah—"He who reveals Himself" as "Strong and Mighty"—a soldier, a warrior, with sufficient power to break down every opposition. Hear Him say, "My presence will go with you to conquer every foe."

*Strong and mighty Lord, give me victory over*
*all the power of the enemy this day. Amen.*

..............................................................................................................................

..............................................................................................................................

..............................................................................................................................

..............................................................................................................................

# Day 22

## The Lord, Mighty in Battle

*Who is this King of glory? . . . the LORD mighty in battle.*
PSALM 24:8

No life can be lived for God in these difficult days without terrific conflict. Foes within and foes without assail each saint continuously. Principalities and powers are arrayed against the child of God who seeks to serve his Master. We have no might with which to meet "this great company that cometh against us" (2 Chronicles 20:12), but the Lord, Mighty in Battle, is our Savior, our Intercessor, our Elder Brother, our ever present Friend.

*"Sure, I must fight if I would win; increase my courage, Lord."* Amen.

.................................................................................................................

.................................................................................................................

.................................................................................................................

.................................................................................................................

# Day 23
## King of Glory

*Who is this King of glory?*
*The LORD of hosts, he is the King of glory.*

PSALM 24:10

Lord Jesus, the glorious King! Not merely a king, but glorious, excelling all others in mighty truth and power, grace and love. We almost forget at times His absolute sovereignty as we bow in humble worship before His matchless glory and cry again and again,

*"Thy Kingdom come," oh Glorious King. Amen.*

.............................................................................................................................

.............................................................................................................................

.............................................................................................................................

.............................................................................................................................

# Day 24

## *My Strong Rock*

*Bow down thine ear to me; deliver me speedily:*
*be thou my strong rock, for an house of defence to save me.*
<small>PSALM 31:2</small>

No sorrow of men is so deep and dark and bitter as to be without a refuge, a rock, a safe retreat. My soul, however deep your sorrow, however dark your sin, however hopeless your lot among men, the Man of Sorrows bore your sin in His own body on the tree. He carried all your grief. He is your "Strong Rock." A strong, safe house, in which I am defended from myself, the world, the devil.

*Rock of ages, cleft for me,*
*Let me hide myself in Thee.*
*Amen.*

.....................................................................................................................

.....................................................................................................................

.....................................................................................................................

.....................................................................................................................

# Day 25

## My Rock and My Fortress

*For thou art my rock and my fortress;*
*therefore for thy name's sake lead me, and guide me.*
PSALM 31:3

Some day our work will all be tried by storm and by fire, and the question will be of our foundation. Are we built on the Rock of Ages, that High Rock which is a Fortress, so that, though the wind blows and the storm shakes all about us, we will stand secure? And if Christ is our "Rock" and our "Fortress" will we build with "wood, hay, {and} stubble" (1 Corinthians 3:12) on *such* an eternal foundation?

*Lord Jesus, may we seek to gather "gold, silver, {and} precious stones," that we may bring some honor to You, our Rock and Fortress, by building what will endure through all the ages. Amen.*

# Day 26

## *The Rock That Is Higher Than I*

*From the end of the earth will I cry unto thee, when my heart is overwhelmed: lead me to the rock that is higher than I.*

PSALM 61:2

*Not down to a dungeon deep,*
*Nor to level of earth, hard by–*
*But lead, when the storm o'erwhelms,*
*To "The Rock That Is Higher Than I."*

*Up from my sin's dark slime,*
*Away from the world's mad cry–*
*To Thee do I come, O Christ!*
*To "The Rock That Is Higher Than I."*

*There will I worship and wait*
*Redeemed, with the saints on high.*
*All glory, and honor, and praise*
*To "The Rock That Is Higher Than I."*

........................................................................................................

........................................................................................................

........................................................................................................

........................................................................................................

# Day 27

## A Strong Tower

*For thou hast been a shelter for me,
and a strong tower from the enemy.*
PSALM 61:3

What is the testimony of *our* souls today as we read what others have said concerning Him who has been a "Strong Tower" from the enemy? Did ever a child of God in danger hurry within the Strong Tower of His Presence and find anything of failure or defeat? Must we not confess that every failure has come when we were found outside?

*Oh Strong Tower, may we enter in today
and dwell in You and be safe.*

......................................................................................................................

......................................................................................................................

......................................................................................................................

......................................................................................................................

# Day 28

## A Stranger and an Alien

*I am become a stranger unto my brethren,*
*and an alien unto my mother's children.*
PSALM 69:8

*What was the price He paid,*
*That, what He bore for me;*
*"A Stranger, an Alien"; alone,*
*He died on Calvary.*

*A "Stranger" to make me a friend,*
*An "Alien" to give me a home.*
*Great Stranger, I fall at Thy feet,*
*No longer from Thee will I roam.*
*Amen.*

.......................................................................................................

.......................................................................................................

.......................................................................................................

.......................................................................................................

# Day 29

## The King's Son

*Give the king thy judgments, O God,*
*and thy righteousness unto the king's son.*
PSALM 72:1

How little do our hearts discern the homage due to God as King and to Jesus as His Son. We bow our heads, we lift our hats, we pay our homage to the fleeting, trifling power of earth's great men, but do we, as we enter the house of God, bow humbly and revere "The King's Son?" Are earthly thoughts hushed and earthly words stilled as we gather in the house of God, and even when our spokesman voices our desires to Him, do wandering thoughts of earthly things deprive us of the blessing and the answer to our prayers?

*Lord, teach us how to pray, that we may truly worship You. Amen.*

.......................................................................................................................

.......................................................................................................................

.......................................................................................................................

.......................................................................................................................

# Day 30

## Rain upon Mown Grass

*He shall come down like rain upon the mown grass.*
PSALM 72:6

*My soul was parched with the fire of sin,*
*My life mowed down with pain,*
*My Savior spoke, "My child, draw near."*
*His word was like the Rain.*

*Refreshing, cleansing, lifting me,*
*My Lord, My All, came down,*
*And now I turn from all earth's dross—*
*To gain a heavenly crown.*

.......................................................................................................................

.......................................................................................................................

.......................................................................................................................

.......................................................................................................................

# Day 31

## *Showers upon the Earth*

*He shall come down. . .as showers that water the earth.*
PSALM 72:6

Our lives grow dusty, dry, and desolate in our earthly pilgrimage, but He who seeks a love that is fresh and pure and strong comes down on us as "the showers that water the earth." Have you turned to Him today and found that cool, refreshing, cleansing blessing which He seeks to give?

*There shall be showers of blessing,*
*Oh, that today they might fall!*
*Now, as to God we're confessing,*
*Now, as on Jesus we call.*
*Amen.*

.......................................................................................................................
.......................................................................................................................
.......................................................................................................................
.......................................................................................................................

# Day 32
## *My Firstborn*

*Also I will make him my firstborn, higher than the kings of the earth.*
PSALM 89:27

"Loose thy shoe from off thy foot; for the place whereon thou standest is holy" (Joshua 5:15). The Eternal Father, God, is speaking. "My Firstborn I will make higher than the kings of earth." Oh, you who are the last-born of the Father, the Firstborn is your Elder Brother. You have shared His humiliation to your salvation. You will share His exaltation to your eternal glory.

*We worship You, Lord Jesus, God's Firstborn! Amen.*

.......................................................................................................................

.......................................................................................................................

.......................................................................................................................

.......................................................................................................................

# Day 33

## The Head Stone of the Corner

*The stone which the builders refused*
*is become the head stone of the corner.*
PSALM 118:22

Men may reject "The Head Stone of the Corner" and seek to erect a building that will stand without the Living Christ. But God has laid aside all human plans and made our Lord and Savior "The Head Stone of the Corner." When all human buildings crumble and every man-taught architect has failed, all hearts bow before that perfect building, that eternal temple, worshipping Him who is its crown of grace.

.................................................................................................................

.................................................................................................................

.................................................................................................................

.................................................................................................................

# Day 34
## *My High Tower*

*My goodness, and my fortress; my high tower, and my deliverer; my shield, and he in whom I trust; who subdueth my people under me.*

PSALM 144:2

"My High Tower" is a vision of our glorious Savior as the Most High—high above our trials; high above our temptations; high above our foes; high above our failures and losses; high above the fret and care of our earthly life. A place of holy calm and peace and stillness. The door is open.

*Lord Jesus, our High Tower, let us enter in today. Amen.*

....................................................................................................

....................................................................................................

....................................................................................................

....................................................................................................

# Day 35

## *Wisdom*

*I wisdom dwell with prudence,
and find out knowledge of witty inventions.*
PROVERBS 8:12

Wisdom is the right use of knowledge. What a wondrous name for Him who gave Himself for us! Who, "when he putteth forth his own sheep, he goeth before them" (John 10:4); who guides us by the skillfulness of His hand.

*May we seek with all our hearts until we find You, and finding You, find Wisdom to do the will of God. Amen.*

.......................................................................................................................

.......................................................................................................................

.......................................................................................................................

.......................................................................................................................

# Day 36

## Excellent

*Let them praise the name of the LORD:*
*for his name alone is excellent.*
PSALM 148:13

"All the glory of the Lord is that in which He excels all others."
"His name alone is excellent," and all His names which represent
some feature of His grace are glorious because they excel any other
name ever uttered among men. What friend, what helper do we know
on earth that ever has or can approach His excellence? And so we turn
with new deep joy to the psalmist's testimony, "They that know thy
name will put their trust in thee" (Psalm 9:10).

.................................................................................................................

.................................................................................................................

.................................................................................................................

.................................................................................................................

# Day 37

## Understanding

*Counsel is mine, and sound wisdom:*
*I am understanding;*
*I have strength.*
PROVERBS 8:14

God is Love, God is Light; God is to us a thousand things for which we long and which we need, but have we realized that in possessing Him and abiding in Him, He is "Understanding," and all that seems dark and difficult will become clear to us as we depend on Him, who is "Understanding"? It would take ten thousand years to learn a few of the many things we long to know on earth. The soul that is linked to God begins to understand and will go on to clearer understanding throughout the countless ages.

.................................................................................................................

.................................................................................................................

.................................................................................................................

.................................................................................................................

# Day 38

## A Friend That Sticketh Closer Than a Brother

*A man that hath friends must shew himself friendly:
and there is a friend that sticketh closer than a brother.*
PROVERBS 18:24

Stay, lonely pilgrim, searching long for fellowship. Stop here and find "A Friend." "There *is* a Friend," though all the world denies it. One who is always true and faithful. One who never leaves and never forsakes. No brother will, or can, abide as He. Will you be a friend to Jesus, as He is a friend to you?

*We worship You, we trust all to You, and we take from You all peace, all grace, all needed power to do and be what pleases You, our never-absent Friend. Amen.*

........................................................................................................

........................................................................................................

........................................................................................................

........................................................................................................

# Day 39

## *Ointment Poured Forth*

*Because of the savour of thy good ointments
thy name is as ointment poured forth.*
SONG OF SOLOMON 1:3

Is your soul sore from sin, from resistance, or from the fiery darts of
Satan, of sinners, or of saints? Then is your Lord to you as "Ointment
Poured Forth," free, abundant, ready, healing, and fragrant. Suffering
soul, come near to Him and let that healing Ointment pour over you
and soothe and heal you.

.......................................................................................................................

.......................................................................................................................

.......................................................................................................................

.......................................................................................................................

# Day 40

## A Bundle of Myrrh

*A bundle of myrrh is my well-beloved unto me.*
SONG OF SOLOMON 4:13

Oh Child of Sorrow, Church of Smyrna, sad soul suffocating in earth's dark vapors, your Lord is for you an exquisite perfume, "A Bundle of Myrrh." A missionary, wearily walking a winding pathway in the night, suddenly came to a spot where the air was heavy with the perfume of wild jasmine and was comforted and refreshed by a fragrance preserved from nonappreciative wild animals and wilder men for a sorrowing toiler. So is your Lord to you "A Bundle of Myrrh."

......................................................................................................

......................................................................................................

......................................................................................................

......................................................................................................

# Day 41

## A Cluster of Camphire

*My beloved is unto me as a cluster of
camphire in the vineyards of Engedi.*
SONG OF SOLOMON 1:14

A beautiful, fragrant flower—"a cluster" of them—exquisite beauty,
exquisite perfume in abundance! Struggling in the midst of experiences that are not fragrant, that are not delightful, have you learned
to turn to Him, who, in the midst of darkness, is Light, in the midst
of battle, is Peace, in the midst of unpleasantness, is to you unlimited
and exquisite delight? Do you know your Lord as "A Cluster of
Camphire"? Acquaint yourself with Him today, and be at peace.

.................................................................................................................

.................................................................................................................

.................................................................................................................

.................................................................................................................

# Day 42

## *The Rose of Sharon*

*I am the rose of Sharon.*
SONG OF SOLOMON 2:1

Child of God, there is no mood of your life where Jesus fails to fit your need, to brighten as a brilliant rose your life. In joy or sorrow, sunshine or shadow, day or night, He blooms for you. Look on Him, then, today, not only on the cross for you, not only on the throne, but near you, close beside your path, "The Rose of Sharon."

.......................................................................................................................

.......................................................................................................................

.......................................................................................................................

.......................................................................................................................

# Day 43
## The Lily of the Valleys

*I am. . .the lily of the valleys.*
SONG OF SOLOMON 2:1

Sweetest, fairest, most exquisite flower that eye has seen, hidden except to eyes that seek it out. So does your Lord unveil Himself to you, even though you walk through the valleys. Only in those deeper shadows can you know His utter loveliness. Look on *Him* then, and "fear no evil."

..............................................................................................................

..............................................................................................................

..............................................................................................................

..............................................................................................................

# Day 44

## Him Whom My Soul Loveth

*I will rise now, and go about the city in the streets,
and in the broad ways I will seek him whom my soul loveth.*
SONG OF SOLOMON 3:2

*Not in the doubting throng,
Not in the boastful song,
But kneeling–with Christ above me–
Humbly I'll say, "I love Thee."*

*Not with my lips alone,
Not for Thy gifts I own,
But just for the grace I see
Jesus, my soul loveth Thee.
Amen.*

...................................................................................................

...................................................................................................

...................................................................................................

...................................................................................................

# Day 45

## The Chiefest among Ten Thousand

*My beloved is white and ruddy, the chiefest among ten thousand.*
SONG OF SOLOMON 5:10

Do we sometimes sing with too little depth of meaning "He's the chiefest of ten thousand to my soul"? Is He really first in our hearts' affection? If so, His presence has been real to us for He has said, "Ye shall seek me, and find me, when ye shall search for me with all your heart," or, "with your whole desire" (Jeremiah 29:13). Here the secret of full transforming communion with our Lord Jesus Christ is found in gazing on Him in all the beauty of His holiness, until in all truthfulness He becomes in our hearts the "Chiefest among Ten Thousand."

...................................................................................................................

...................................................................................................................

...................................................................................................................

...................................................................................................................

# Day 46
## *Altogether Lovely*

*His mouth is most sweet: yea, he is altogether lovely.*
SONG OF SOLOMON 5:16

*Every earthly joy will pall,*
*Every earthly friend will fall.*
*Only Christ is to the end*
*"Altogether Lovely," Friend.*

*Do you see His wondrous face?*
*Full of glory, love, and grace?*
*Look, and all thy need confess,*
*Worship His pure Holiness.*

...................................................................................................................

...................................................................................................................

...................................................................................................................

...................................................................................................................

# Day 47
## The Branch of the Lord

*In that day shall the branch of the LORD be beautiful and glorious.*
ISAIAH 4:2

By every means and picture which we can understand, the Spirit reveals our Savior's oneness with God. None is more clear or full of meaning to us than this, "The Branch of the Lord." One with the Father, growing out of and yet a part of Him. And we are "branches" of Christ (see John 15). As we worship the Christ who is very God, we hear Him say, "If ye abide in me. . .ye shall ask what ye will, and it shall be done unto you" (John 15:7).

.......................................................................................................................

.......................................................................................................................

.......................................................................................................................

.......................................................................................................................

# Day 48

## *Jehovah of Hosts*

*And one cried unto another, and said, Holy, holy, holy,
is the LORD of hosts: the whole earth is full of his glory.*
ISAIAH 6:3

The "Jehovah" of the Old Testament is the "Jesus" of the New. If we always think (as Scofield suggested) of Jehovah as "God revealing Himself," and the words of Jehovah-Jesus, "Blessed are the pure in heart: for they shall see God" (Matthew 5:8), then will the heavens around us be always full of the chariots and horsemen of Jehovah of Hosts, and all fear will be stilled and His revelation of Himself to us will not be in vain.

*Lord Jesus, Jehovah of hosts, give us a vision of Your glory
this day. Amen.*

.................................................................................................

.................................................................................................

.................................................................................................

.................................................................................................

# Day 49
## *The Child*

*For before the child shall know to refuse the evil, and choose the good,*
*the land that thou abhorrest shall be forsaken of both her kings.*
ISAIAH 7:16

The first, last, and foremost mark of Christ's deity was His great
humility. The greatest Sage and Seer of all the ages, "A Child"! The
Everlasting God, hoary-white with eternal years, "A Child"! Then will
*we* hesitate to "become as little children," knowing that only childlike
will we enter the kingdom?

..........................................................................................................................

..........................................................................................................................

..........................................................................................................................

..........................................................................................................................

# Day 50

## A Sanctuary

*And he shall be for a sanctuary.*
ISAIAH 8:14

Where is your place of worship? Where, in the turmoil of the street; where, in the busy cares of home; where, in the hurry and confusion of men, will our souls find the place to pray? "He shall be for a 'Sanctuary,' closer to thee than breathing, nearer than hands or feet." At any moment during all the hurried day you may be hidden from all earth's eyes and quiet from all earth's clamor. Only abide in Him.

...................................................................................................................................

...................................................................................................................................

...................................................................................................................................

...................................................................................................................................

# Day 54

## *A Great Light*

*The people that walked in darkness have seen a great light:*
*they that dwell in the land of the shadow of death,*
*upon them hath the light shined.*

ISAIAH 9:2

It is the people who once walked in darkness who are able to see the greatness of the light. It is the soul which finds that it is lost that seeks the Lord. Have *you* seen the Light? The beloved apostle said, "That which we have seen and heard declare we unto you. . . . This then is the message which we. . .declare unto you, that God is light, and in him is no darkness" (1 John 1:3, 5).

*Lord, let my life and lips tell the story of the Light my eyes*
*have seen. Amen.*

# Day 52
## *Wonderful*

*For unto us a child is born, unto us a son is given. . .*
*and his name shall be called Wonderful.*
ISAIAH 9:6

Jesus is "the same yesterday, today, and forever," and men who think Him commonplace or at most only an unusual man will sometime stand ashamed and confounded as they hear this prophecy fulfilled, "His name shall be called Wonderful." Today He is working just as wonderful works as when He created the heaven and the earth. His wondrous grace, His wonderful omnipotence, is for His child who needs Him and who trusts Him, even today. Attempt great things for God and expect great things from Him, and you will begin even now to say, His name is Wonderful.

.................................................................................................................

.................................................................................................................

.................................................................................................................

.................................................................................................................

# Day 53
## *Counsellor*

*For unto us a child is born, unto us a son is given. . .*
*and his name shall be called. . .Counsellor.*
ISAIAH 9:6

Not often is He called "Counsellor" now. Even God's saints
continuously ask of men instead of God, "How may I find God's
will?" Conference after conference is held by both the world and
the church to find by human wisdom some better plan for earthly
government, or for the church, or for the welfare of our earthly life
and walk. But how rarely do we bow together or alone to seek that
heavenly wisdom, that divine counsel, which alone will enable us to
find our way out of the mazes in which we wander. When will His
Name be joyfully and triumphantly proclaimed as "Counsellor" by
His people? By you?

....................................................................................................................

....................................................................................................................

....................................................................................................................

....................................................................................................................

# Day 54
## *The Mighty God*

*For unto us a child is born, unto us a son is given. . .*
*and his name shall be called. . .The mighty God.*
ISAIAH 9:6

Have we doubted His might and feared in the day when some foe
was near? Listen! His name is "The Mighty God." Do away with all
doubt and fear! "Thou hast made the heaven and the earth. . .there is
nothing too hard for thee" (Jeremiah 32:17).

*Lord, I bow to the dust and worship.*
*Mighty God, show Your power in me! Amen.*

.......................................................................................................................

.......................................................................................................................

.......................................................................................................................

.......................................................................................................................

# Day 55
## *The Everlasting Father*

*For unto us a child is born, unto us a son is given. . .*
*and his name shall be called. . .The everlasting Father.*
ISAIAH 9:6

Who has not mourned a father's death and felt the loss of his transient power and helpfulness? The Child who was born in Bethlehem, who gave His life for you, is not only your Savior and your King, but "His name shall be called The Everlasting Father." In His everlasting love, within His everlasting arms, within His Father-heart which pities you—His child—you will find safety, rest, and comfort.

...........................................................................................................................................

...........................................................................................................................................

...........................................................................................................................................

...........................................................................................................................................

# Day 56

## *The Prince of Peace*

*For unto us a child is born, unto us a son is given. . .*
*and his name shall be called. . .The Prince of Peace.*
ISAIAH 9:6

He who proclaimed to loyal hearts, "Peace I leave with you, my peace I give unto you: not as the world giveth, give I unto you" (John 14:27), is rightly called "The Prince of Peace." He who brought such peace to earth was rejected of men and waits still to be crowned on earth; but He gives before that royal day a peace that surpasses understanding to every trusting heart. Have you received it? Will you, in loyalty to "The Prince of Peace," accept in humble faith His peace today?

.......................................................................................................................

.......................................................................................................................

.......................................................................................................................

.......................................................................................................................

# Day 57

## The Light of Israel

*And the light of Israel shall be for a fire,*
*and his Holy One for a flame: and it shall burn*
*and devour his thorns and his briers in one day.*

ISAIAH 10:17

Jesus was and is the "Light of Israel." He is also the "Light of life" and the "Light of men," a "Light to lighten the world." But the "Light of Israel" was "to burn and devour thorns and briers." Dear child of God, are you bringing the useless branches, the unpleasant, unlovely things of your life into the Light of His Presence that they may be consumed? Some day the shining of His Presence will destroy the devil himself. Will we not submit our lives to that Wondrous Light and ask Him to consume all evil in us?

............................................................................................................

............................................................................................................

............................................................................................................

............................................................................................................

# Day 58

## A Rod out of the Stem of Jesse

*And there shall come forth a rod out of the stem of Jesse,*
*and a Branch shall grow out of his roots.*

ISAIAH 44:4

Only a "rod" from a human "stem"? Only a "root" from "dry
ground"? Has He no "form nor comeliness," no "beauty that we
should desire"? "Surely He bore our griefs" and the way of "our
peace" was in Him. "Because He stooped so low God hath exalted
Him very high," and the beauty of a tender plant was the glory of God
on high.

.......................................................................................................................

.......................................................................................................................

.......................................................................................................................

.......................................................................................................................

# Day 59

## A Branch out of His Roots

*And there shall come forth a rod out of the stem of Jesse,*
*and a Branch shall grow out of his roots.*

ISAIAH 11:1

Of all the miracles that attest to the deity of our Lord, including the miraculous preservation of the scriptures, none is more wonderful or convincing to the honest, faithful heart than the preservation, not only of Israel, but of that section of Israel, humble in its origin, which revealed our Lord to be born of the family of David and of Jesse. Out of the nations scattered over the earth, out of the line of kings who long had ceased to reign, there came, as the prophet said, a "Branch out of His Roots" of the stem of Jesse. And He who was of the seed of David will just as surely come again to reign once more over Israel, and through Israel, over all the earth.

*Lord, our faint hearts believe once more in*
*God's eternal truth and faithfulness. Amen.*

.................................................................................................................

.................................................................................................................

.................................................................................................................

.................................................................................................................

# Day 60

## *The Root of Jesse*

*And in that day there shall be a root of Jesse. . .*
*to it shall the Gentiles seek: and his rest shall be glorious.*
ISAIAH 11:10

It is not Israel alone who will rejoice when "a root of Jesse. . .shall stand for an ensign of the people," for "to it shall the Gentiles seek," and all the gracious promises and gifts God gave to Jesse and to David and his seed which could bring rest and comfort to our souls belong to us who worship Jesus, David's Son, and Jesse's Root. How all the grace and glory of our God through all the ages is gathered up for us who from the Gentile world bow at His feet and find His glorious rest!

.................................................................................................

.................................................................................................

.................................................................................................

.................................................................................................

# Day 64

## *The Ensign of the People*

*And in that day there shall be a root of Jesse,*
*which shall stand for an ensign of the people.*
ISAIAH 11:10

Jesus is the people's flag, an "Ensign of the People." Wherever and whenever He is lifted up the people seek after Him. Is not our failure to win many to the Lord due to our misrepresentation of Him? To our failure to reveal the beauty of His holiness and to enter into His glorious rest? Will we bow in humble confession while we pray that we who are His representatives may be saved from misrepresentation of Him by lives that are cruelly unlike Him and seek for grace to exalt Him everywhere among men?

.......................................................................................................................

.......................................................................................................................

.......................................................................................................................

.......................................................................................................................

# Day 62

## *My Strength and My Song*

*Behold, God is my salvation; I will trust, and not be afraid:
for the LORD JEHOVAH is my strength and my song;
he also is become my salvation.*

ISAIAH 12:2

We know Jehovah is our "Strength," but do we make Him also our
"Song"? As we make Him our song and sing of Him, we lose our fear.
We are able to "trust and not be afraid," only as we *sing* of Him. Our
Redeemer *is* our "Strength." Make Him your "Song" today.

......................................................................................................................

......................................................................................................................

......................................................................................................................

......................................................................................................................

# Day 63

## A Nail Fastened in a Sure Place

*And I will fasten him as a nail in a sure place.*
ISAIAH 22:23

Men have dreamed fantastic ideas concerning Christ as a "Nail in a Sure Place." Whatever else this name may or may not mean, it brings to the worshipping child of God a sense of the fixedness, the certainty and security of Jesus Christ in His relationship to the temple and throne of God. If we on earth are being built together for a dwelling place of God, yet more sure is the fact of the presence of Christ filling the house. If we are "pillars who go no more out," it is because He is secure—His place is "fastened" and "sure." "So shall we ever be with the Lord" (1 Thessalonians 4:17), for where He is, there will His servant be also, and our abiding is as sure as Christ's.

# Day 64

## A Glorious Throne to His Father's House

*He shall be for a glorious throne to his father's house.*
ISAIAH 22:23

One of the most vivid pictures painted by the Holy Spirit of the life that lies beyond follows in the Revelation—the swift, wondrous vision of the church on earth (Revelation 4:2–3). "Behold, a throne ⁅was⁆ set in heaven. . .and there was a rainbow round about the throne." That rainbow brings us hope and comfort and the precious, glorious promise that our Lord Himself is a "Glorious Throne to His Father's House." Let it be no longer hard or difficult for you to pray. The throne that you bow before is not one of austere justice but rather one of infinite grace. Let us therefore come boldly to the Throne of Grace that we may obtain mercy and find help.

# Day 65

## *Strength to the Poor and Needy*

*For thou hast been a strength to the poor,
a strength to the needy in his distress.*
ISAIAH 25:4

Touched with the feeling of our infirmities, our Lord in His omnipotence becomes a "Strength to the Poor and Needy." Let us never forget that His strength is made perfect in our weakness only when we realize our helplessness and fling ourselves, as trusting children, into the outstretched arms by which He "created the heavens and the earth." With what a wondrous picture does our Lord reveal Himself as the supply for our every need and "strength to the poor"!

.......................................................................................................................

.......................................................................................................................

.......................................................................................................................

.......................................................................................................................

# Day 66

## A Shadow from the Heat

*For thou hast been. . .a shadow from the heat.*
ISAIAH 25:4

In the intolerable heat of the sun as it beats down on the plateaus of equatorial Africa, one may step from the unbearable heat to a shade so cool, so refreshing, that until it is experienced it is almost beyond conception or belief. Our Lord pictures Himself to His weary, toiling children, struggling onward in the heat of almost impossible experiences, as a "Shadow from the Heat," into whose presence we may step at any moment of our pilgrimage and find cool, refreshing rest.

.......................................................................................................................

.......................................................................................................................

.......................................................................................................................

.......................................................................................................................

# Day 67

## A Refuge from the Storm

*For thou hast been. . .a refuge from the storm. . .*
*when the blast of the terrible ones is as a storm against the wall.*

ISAIAH 25:4

"God is faithful, who will not suffer you to be tempted above that
ye are able; but will with the temptation, also make a way to escape,"
a "refuge from the storm," "that ye may be able to bear it"
(1 Corinthians 10:13). It is necessary that we pass through storms
and that we feel their force and chilling blast, for only in such
experiences could we ever know the comfort, the witness, of Him
who is our "Refuge from the Storm." Are we hiding in Him?

.................................................................................................

.................................................................................................

.................................................................................................

.................................................................................................

# Day 68

## The Rock of Ages

*Trust ye in the LORD for ever: for in the LORD JEHOVAH
is everlasting strength. ⸗Margin note: "Rock of Ages"⸗*
ISAIAH 26:4

Many of the college buildings at Oxford University, hundreds of years
old, were described by one who studied there more than half a century
ago as "leprous with age." Many stones are crumbling away, and some
must be replaced to save the buildings. The strongest rocks in which
men hide the bodies of departed friends are often broken apart by a
growing plant. But He who calls us to "trust in Jehovah forever" calls
Himself "An Everlasting Rock" or "The Rock of Ages." Let us trust in
Him today, tomorrow, and forever.

......................................................................................................................................

......................................................................................................................................

......................................................................................................................................

......................................................................................................................................

# Day 69

## A Crown of Glory

*In that day shall the LORD of hosts be for a crown of glory.*
ISAIAH 28:5

We hear and think much of redeemed and fruitful saints shining as stars in the diadem of our Lord, but in this wondrous title of our glorious Savior we have a new vision of His relationship to His people. Souls who have been downtrodden and scorned by those the world calls great will in that day, as He honors redeemed believers as His bride, find that the presence, the tender and gracious love of the King of Glory, will be to them in the eyes of all, a witness, a "Crown of Glory." Oh, you who are redeemed from among the lost, who was dead and are alive, was lost and are found, look upon His wondrous grace! The King of kings, the Lord of lords, will be to you a Crown of Glory. Then fall at His feet today and worship Him with all your heart.

.........................................................................................................

.........................................................................................................

.........................................................................................................

.........................................................................................................

# Day 70

## A Diadem of Beauty

*In that day shall the LORD of hosts be. . .*
*for a diadem of beauty, unto the residue of his people.*
ISAIAH 28:5

The difference between a Crown of Glory and a "Diadem of Beauty" is that in the first the excellence, the worth, the value, the glory of God will be on the saints. While in the other, the beauty, the very radiance of the Lord, will fill and shine out from those who, in a moment, in the twinkling of an eye, will be changed into His likeness. Oh humble child of God, see the exceeding grace which will be revealed in the ages to come. The beauty of the Lord our God will be on you, and He will be to you a crown or Diadem of Beauty. He "that hath this hope in him purifieth himself" (1 John 3:3).

........................................................................................................

........................................................................................................

........................................................................................................

........................................................................................................

# Day 71

## *The Foundation*

*Therefore thus saith the Lord GOD,*
*Behold, I lay in Zion for a foundation.*
ISAIAH 28:16

Of all the gracious promises concerning the children of God, none is more wonderful than that which describes the saints as polished stones in the temple where He dwells. With divine grace our Lord calls Himself "The Foundation," an "Everlasting Rock," "The Rock of Ages." Where stands our faith today? Are we building on the sands of human philosophies or on Him?

*On the Rock of Ages founded,*
*Naught can shake our sure repose.*

.........................................................................................................................................

.........................................................................................................................................

.........................................................................................................................................

.........................................................................................................................................

# Day 72

## A Sure Foundation

*Therefore thus saith the Lord GOD, Behold,*
*I lay in Zion. . .a sure foundation.*
ISAIAH 28:16

All the chiseling, all the polishing of experiences through which we pass, is costly. Will it last? Is it worthwhile? Worthwhile to suffer on and say, "Dear Lord, prevent not Your hand to comfort us and steady us"? Through just such testing times the Master calls Himself a "Sure Foundation." No experiment here, no doubt, no room for anxious thought or fear. He who builds on that "Sure Foundation" finds his building secure, and he will be a "pillar in the temple of God," to "go no more out forever."

.................................................................................................

.................................................................................................

.................................................................................................

.................................................................................................

# Day 73

## A Tried Stone

*Therefore thus saith the Lord GOD, Behold,*
*I lay in Zion. . . a tried stone.*

ISAIAH 28:16

How strange is this experience of our Lord. Surely the Father knew
the Son, knew His every capacity and power. Yet He was tried by
God as we need to be tried, only that He might leave us an "example
that we might walk in His steps." What mockery, what hopeless
blasphemy, that He should be rejected by some builders! Let us ask
the great Master Builder to test us and to chisel us until we fit in the
place which He has prepared for us.

.......................................................................................................................

.......................................................................................................................

.......................................................................................................................

.......................................................................................................................

# Day 74

## A Covert from the Tempest

*And a man shall be as. . .a covert from the tempest.*
ISAIAH 32:2

Of no other being could such language be used, in no other literature of the world is such marvelous imagery to be found, as that used in the Word of God to picture the grace and glory of our Lord. When the destructive tempests sweep and we hide in Him, will we be safe? He will be a "Covert from the Tempest"—covered, sheltered, safe. Are we hiding in Him?

.......................................................................................................................

.......................................................................................................................

.......................................................................................................................

.......................................................................................................................

# Day 75

## *As a Hiding Place from the Wind*

*And a man shall be as an hiding place from the wind.*
ISAIAH 32:2

Standing one day on the deck of a steamer in the harbor at Aden, a traveler saw a storm of wind sweeping across the desert like some high, mountainous wave, rolling and sweeping forward until it struck the sea and lashed it to foam. Then on across the bay until it struck ships lying there at anchor, till nearly every boat was torn from its moorings or forced to loosen every cable and steam with full force into the face of the terrific wind. No hiding place was there. So do the storms of hate, of evil, and of sin sweep over our lives as we journey toward our everlasting home. But for every soul who knows his own helplessness, our Savior is Himself a "Hiding Place from the Wind."

.......................................................................................................................

.......................................................................................................................

.......................................................................................................................

.......................................................................................................................

# Day 76

## *Shadow of a Great Rock in a Weary Land*

*And a man shall be as. . .the shadow of a great rock in a weary land.*
ISAIAH 32:2

Journeying one night in the wilderness of central Africa in a section plagued by many ravenous beasts, we found no place of safety till we came to the shadow of a great rock, where we sat down with our backs to the rock and, building at our feet a great fire, found rest and were refreshed for the next day's still weary journey. Oh weary child, when your strength fails and you can go no farther, sit down and lean back in the shadow of your Lord, on Him. Build there in prayer the fire of faith and find rest and refreshment for your onward march.

........................................................................................................................................

........................................................................................................................................

........................................................................................................................................

........................................................................................................................................

# Day 77
## As Rivers of Water in a Dry Place

*And a man shall be as. . .rivers of water in a dry place.*
ISAIAH 32:2

To know the blessing of water in abundance, we need to have felt a very intense thirst. Wandering one time in part of Africa's desert, two missionaries traveled without water until thirst became first a pain, then an agony, then almost insanity. After long marching over dry, burning sands they came to the waters of a wide, deep river and quenched their thirst. "If any man thirst, let him come unto me" (John 7:37) and He is near. No matter how deep our thirst, how great our longing or our need, He who is as "Rivers of Water in a Dry Place" has said, "Lo, I am with you. Drink, and be satisfied."

.............................................................................................................

.............................................................................................................

.............................................................................................................

.............................................................................................................

# Day 78
## The King in His Beauty

*Thine eyes shall see the king in his beauty:*
*they shall behold the land that is very far off.*
ISAIAH 33:17

"Blessed are the pure in heart: for they shall see God" (Matthew 5:8). Do our lives see the King in His beauty? Do we grip the fact that as we gaze on Him it is His will that we should be transformed into His likeness, "from glory unto glory"? "A little while, and the world seeth me no more; but ye see me" (John 14:19). No more wonderful promise is ours for present experiences than this.

*Oh Lord, let every mist and veil that hides Your glory be removed, and every sin be put away, that we may see You in the beauty of holiness. Then "the beauty of the Lord thy God shall be upon thee."*

.................................................................................................

.................................................................................................

.................................................................................................

.................................................................................................

# Day 79
## *Our Lawgiver*

*For the LORD is our judge, the LORD is our lawgiver,
the LORD is our king; he will save us.*
ISAIAH 33:22

Every nation, every act, every life, needs a law to direct it in its relation to its own expression and to others. That law must be made by one who knows and understands the nation, act, or life. Jesus is our "Lawgiver." He who gave us life, He who has lived the life we need to live—He knows. He made the law for us in infinite tenderness and love. "He that hath my commandments, and keepeth them, he it is that loveth me" (John 14:24).

...................................................................................................................................

...................................................................................................................................

...................................................................................................................................

...................................................................................................................................

# Day 80

## *Jehovah*

*The voice of one that crieth, Prepare ye in the wilderness the way*
*of Jehovah; make level in the desert a highway for our God.*
ISAIAH 40:3 ASV

Jehovah—"The Self-existent One who reveals Himself." Into the
wilderness of my lost way He comes to find me and lead me out. Into
the desert of my barren life enters Jehovah and makes all the desert
a garden. Into my death He brings His life and to my dead senses
reveals Himself as The One Eternal God. Will we not bow before
His Majesty and worship Jehovah, while we pray for greater grace to
receive all the revelation of Himself which He would give?

........................................................................................................

........................................................................................................

........................................................................................................

........................................................................................................

# Day 84

## The Lord Jehovah

*Behold, the Lord Jehovah will come as a mighty one,
and his arm will rule for him: Behold, his reward is with him,
and his recompense before him.*

ISAIAH 40:10 ASV

Not every soul that worships Jehovah has learned that the secret of all power and of fullness of blessing is in making Him the Master of our lives. Adonai Jehovah is the Lord, the Ruler, the Master, who in eternal grace reveals Himself. Will we not humbly bow at His feet and crown Him Lord, Master, of all that we have and are?

.......................................................................................................................................

.......................................................................................................................................

.......................................................................................................................................

.......................................................................................................................................

# Day 82

## The Everlasting God

*Hast thou not known? hast thou not heard, that the everlasting God,
the LORD, the Creator of the ends of the earth, fainteth not,
neither is weary? there is no searching of his understanding.*

ISAIAH 40:28

*Everlasting, never-ending,*
*Age-abiding is my Lord.*
*Never shadow caused by turning,*
*Changeless, perfect, is His Word.*

*Everlasting God, I pray Thee*
*Steady, strengthen, stablish me.*
*Safe from grief and pain and failure,*
*Hide me, Everlasting God, in Thee.*

.........................................................................................................................

.........................................................................................................................

.........................................................................................................................

.........................................................................................................................

# Day 83
## Light of the Gentiles

*I the LORD have called thee in righteousness,*
*and will. . .give thee. . .for a light of the Gentiles.*
ISAIAH 42:6

"In him was life; and the life was the light of men" (John 1:4). But how will that Light lighten the Gentiles unless we who are the light of the world go out among the Gentiles and let the light shine? Someone brought that Light to us. Will we not carry it on a little farther into the darkness of some other life? He *is* the Light. He *gave* the Light. *We* are the *Light-bearers*.

.......................................................................................................................

.......................................................................................................................

.......................................................................................................................

.......................................................................................................................

# Day 84
## Mine Elect

*Behold my servant, whom I uphold; mine elect,*
*in whom my soul delighteth; I have put my spirit upon him:*
*he shall bring forth judgment to the Gentiles.*
ISAIAH 42:1

Infinite God, who knows and understands, the God of wisdom and of knowledge, called in review all angels and all men of all the ages and of all time and chose our Lord and called Him "Mine Elect," to be the world's Redeemer, Savior, Friend, and the believer's All in All. Does your choice fall on Him, each day, each hour, in each experience? May He be all in all to you today.

.................................................................................................................................

.................................................................................................................................

.................................................................................................................................

.................................................................................................................................

# Day 85
## *The Polished Shaft*

*And he hath made my mouth like a sharp sword;*
*in the shadow of his hand hath he hid me,*
*and made me a polished shaft; in his quiver hath he hid me.*
ISAIAH 49:2

In every part of the Word of God our Lord is pictured as the "Word
of God" having a "voice as the sound of many waters" (Revelation
4:15), and speaking to His people words of peace and comfort and
of power. But no name of Christ is truer of Him than that He is a
"Polished Shaft," and when He speaks and His word cuts through
our selfish lives like a sword of radiant light, let us rejoice. The devil
would make us proud of self. Few human friends are faithful, but He
who is "A Polished Shaft" speaks not only with eternal love but with
unchanging faithfulness.

*"Speak Lord, for thy servant heareth thee."* Amen.

.......................................................................................................

.......................................................................................................

.......................................................................................................

.......................................................................................................

# Day 86
## The Holy One of Israel

*Thus saith the Lord, the Redeemer of Israel, and his Holy One,
to him whom man despiseth, to him whom the nation abhorreth,
to a servant of rulers, Kings shall see and arise, princes also shall
worship, because of the Lord that is faithful, and the Holy One
of Israel, and he shall choose thee.*

Isaiah 49:7

All Israel walked in sin. All Israel was defiled. And yet in cloud
by day, in fire by night, within the Holy tabernacle there stood a
Presence, holy, infinite in love and grace and power. "The Holy One
of Israel" could not forget His chosen people nor resist their faintest
cry. So Israel stood and lived, and lives today because "The Holy One
of Israel" stood beside them. And beside your soul He stands today
to be your righteousness and lead you to Himself. Look on Him and
adore!

.......................................................................................................................

.......................................................................................................................

.......................................................................................................................

.......................................................................................................................

# Day 87

## A Root out of a Dry Ground

*For he shall grow up before him as a tender plant,*
*and as a root out of a dry ground.*
ISAIAH 53:2

Dear discouraged soul, does it seem sometimes to you that your lot is a hard one? That you have been asked to stand in difficult places and where surrounding conditions have been extremely unfavorable? He who redeemed you knows every difficulty, every sorrow, which you can feel. Dishonored by ignorant doubters, He had to turn even to the wondrous mother who had received both natural and supernatural knowledge of His divine character and mission and ask, "How is it that ye sought me? wist ye not. . . ?" (Luke 2:49). He has suffered "in all points like as we" and is, therefore, "able to succor" us. Then "consider him who grew up A Root Out of a Dry Ground," in case you grow weary and faint in your minds.

.................................................................................................................

.................................................................................................................

.................................................................................................................

.................................................................................................................

# Day 88

## A Man of Sorrows

*He is despised and rejected of men; a man of sorrows,*
*and acquainted with grief: and we hid as it were our faces from him;*
*he was despised, and we esteemed him not.*

ISAIAH 53:3

He who was the source of all joy, the giver of all peace, He before whom angels and archangels bow in adoration, is also called a "Man of Sorrows." Grief broke His heart, crushed out His life. Will we through disobedience, rebellion, or lack of love or service, or worship, add to the sorrows which He bore; or will we murmur if we, too, will be permitted to partake of His sorrows, or to share His grief? He sorrowed all alone, except perhaps as angels ministered to Him in Gethsemane's deep shadow. But He shares your grief; He carries all your sorrow and comforts those who trust in Him. Will we not worship and adore the Man of Sorrows?

.............................................................................................................................

.............................................................................................................................

.............................................................................................................................

.............................................................................................................................

# Day 89

## *My Righteous Servant*

*He shall see of the travail of his soul, and shall be satisfied:*
*by his knowledge shall my righteous servant justify many;*
*for he shall bear their iniquities.*

ISAIAH 53:11

There are many servants; only One is righteous. Paul was able to say,
"I have declared unto you the whole counsel of God, I have fought
a good fight, I have kept the faith," but still must call himself an
unprofitable servant, and less than the least of all saints. Will we
therefore become discouraged and conclude that it is not worthwhile
to try? No, "your labor is not in vain in the Lord," for He who was
"My Righteous Servant shall justify many." For He is still "Jehovah
Tsidkenu" (our Righteousness), and we may bring the dropped
stitches of our best weaving, and the broken efforts of our best service,
and laying all at His feet rejoice that we are justified by Him who is
God's "Righteous Servant."

.......................................................................................................................

.......................................................................................................................

.......................................................................................................................

.......................................................................................................................

# Day 90
## *My Maker*

*For thy Maker is thine husband.*
ISAIAH 54:5

We hear of "self-made men," of men who are made by their surroundings, or of men who are made by devoted friends and companions. How rarely do we hear today the humble, joyful boast, "By the grace of God I am what I am." And yet "He is thy Maker"! All you are that is lasting, all you are that is good, all you are that is helpful, God has made. Bow then before your Maker. Worship and petition Him to finish what He began.

.................................................................................................................................

.................................................................................................................................

.................................................................................................................................

.................................................................................................................................

# Day 94

## *The God of the Whole Earth*

*The LORD of hosts is his name; and thy Redeemer the Holy One of Israel; The God of the whole earth shall he be called.*
ISAIAH 54:5

Is there any part of the earth that is mine? Not till I am truly a child of "The God of the Whole Earth." May I not receive Him and possess all things in Christ and proceed to enjoy them, untroubled by the world's woe? Not till the whole earth has heard that He is "The God," not of a few, but "of the whole earth."

.............................................................................................................................

.............................................................................................................................

.............................................................................................................................

.............................................................................................................................

# Day 92

## *A Witness to the People*

*Behold, I have given him for a witness to the people.*
ISAIAH 55:4

A witness of the love of God, the grace, the power, the holiness of deity. No flaw in all that matchless testimony, no doubtful, double-meaning speech, and He could say, "He that hath seen me hath seen the Father" (John 14:9). We, too, are witnesses, but oh, how full of flaws is all our testimony! The Father dwelled with Him, and He sought the Father's guidance at every step and every word. We, too, may see and hear and walk with God, and so alone will our witness win the wanderers home.

.......................................................................................................................

.......................................................................................................................

.......................................................................................................................

.......................................................................................................................

# Day 93

## *A Leader*

*Behold, I have given him for. . .a leader. . .to the people.*
Isaiah 55:4

From the beginning of our Christian lives the fact that "He leadeth me" is one of the most blessed thoughts that comes to a child of God. But we think most often of His leading us to battle, leading us out of the mazes of confusion and ignorance, leading us through the darkness of our night. Do we realize that infinite tenderness that makes Him gently lead those who are doing the finest and the most difficult and unknown service of the world? The sorrow, the loneliness, the pain, which no friend on earth can know, He understands, He feels with us, and gently leads us through the shadows to His own great glory. Will we not follow where He leads and keep so close to Him that we will never miss the way?

...........................................................................................................

...........................................................................................................

...........................................................................................................

...........................................................................................................

# Day 94

## A Commander

*Behold, I have given him for a. . .commander to the people.*
ISAIAH 55:4

In a day when nearly every man desires to do what is right in his own eyes, it becomes difficult for all of God's children to recognize His right to command. Yet He who redeemed us, who bought us so that we are not our own, proclaimed His right to the title of "Commander." Failure to obey will account for most of the loss of communion and joy in prayer and in the study of God's Word. If there is any commandment which He has brought home to our hearts which we have not obeyed, will we not today grant Him instant, cheerful, loving obedience, and make Him in every detail of life our Commander?

..............................................................................................

..............................................................................................

..............................................................................................

..............................................................................................

# Day 95

## The Redeemer

*And the Redeemer shall come to Zion, and unto them that turn from transgression in Jacob, saith the LORD.*
ISAIAH 59:20

When failure comes and disappointment, when your soul has been defeated and the race seems hopeless, stop and think "thy Lord redeemed thee and at countless cost." If He saw in you something worth paying His life, Himself, His all, is it not worthwhile to rise and try again, walking with Him and worshipping Him who redeemed you?

.................................................................................................................................

.................................................................................................................................

.................................................................................................................................

.................................................................................................................................

# Day 96

## Thine Everlasting Light

*Thy sun shall no more go down; neither shall thy moon
withdraw itself: for the LORD shall be thine everlasting light,
and the days of thy mourning shall be ended.*
ISAIAH 60:20

No picture is more difficult for us to spiritually comprehend than a
time when the sun will no longer go down. When Christ will be to us
"Everlasting Light." Our lives are so filled with ups and downs, with
lights and shadows, that stability seems almost inconceivable, and
everlasting darkness easier to understand than everlasting light. Yet
such is Christ to you. Then enter in with holy boldness and walk in
Everlasting Light.

........................................................................................................

........................................................................................................

........................................................................................................

........................................................................................................

# Day 97

## The Angel of His Presence

*In all their affliction he was afflicted, and the angel of his presence saved them: in his love and in his pity he redeemed them; and he bare them, and carried them all the days of old.*

ISAIAH 63:9

A nervous, restless boy, in his early childhood, called out again and again in the night, "Daddy, are you there?" The father answered, "Yes, I am here. Do you want anything?" "No, I only wanted to be sure you were there." And the frightened boy, still in the dark, went immediately to sleep. Oh child of God, overwhelmed by fears and troubled so that you have found no rest, let "The Angel of His Presence" comfort you. Uncover your ears. Speak to Him, and you will hear the voice of Him who spoke as man never spoke, saying "Lo, I am with thee."

.........................................................................................................

.........................................................................................................

.........................................................................................................

.........................................................................................................

# Day 98

## *Our Potter*

*But now, O LORD, thou art our father; we are the clay,
and thou our potter; and we all are the work of thy hand.*
ISAIAH 64:8

Have you understood the meaning of the force that presses in on your life today? Has it seemed only pain, only wrong and deep injustice? Behind all that seems to be that the Potter *stands*, with an ideal so lofty that our highest imagination has not fully grasped it. A beauteous, transformed life, fit to sit with Him on His throne, is in the Potter's mind, and He is shaping you through what seems a rude experience. Will we not learn to say today,

> *"I am the clay, and Thou the Potter.
> Shape me as Thou wilt, dear Lord."* Amen.

# Day 99

## *Balm of Gilead*

*Is there no balm in Gilead?*
JEREMIAH 8:22

There are experiences of suffering through which the Master wills that we should pass. There are burdens which He does not lift, though He takes us, burden and all, into His everlasting arms. But in every suffering which He permits, He is our "Balm." He eases every pain. He comforts every sorrow. He strengthens us in every weakness. There is a "Balm" in our Gilead. Will we take from Him the comfort which He offers us today?

.............................................................................................................................

.............................................................................................................................

.............................................................................................................................

.............................................................................................................................

# Day 100

## My Physician

*Is there no physician {in Gilead}? why then is not the health of the daughter of my people recovered?*
JEREMIAH 8:22

Dr. Arthur T. Pierson once said in a sermon preached in London, England, that one of the marked proofs of our failure to live up to the light we have is found in our failure to obey the commandment in James's epistle, "Is any sick among you? let him call for the elders of the church; and let them pray over him" (James 5:14). We rush at once to secure human aid, forgetting even to pray as we go, or that He who formed us and through whose blessing alone human efforts can be effective is "Our Physician."

........................................................................................................

........................................................................................................

........................................................................................................

........................................................................................................

# Day 104

## My Portion

*The portion of Jacob is not like them: for he is the former
of all things; and Israel is the rod of his inheritance:
The LORD of hosts is his name.*

JEREMIAH 10:16

When we are able to lay hold of the fact that Jesus is "Our Portion,"
then do we truly possess all things, for "how shall he not with him
also freely give us all things?" (Romans 8:32) No, more, "For all
things are your's. Whether Paul, or Apollos, or Cephas, or the world,
or life, or death, or things present, or things to come; all are your's;
And ye are Christ's; and Christ is God's" (1 Corinthians 3:21-23).
Will we seek to take hold of all of His matchless love and grace and
hope and courage and joy and fruit and power? What more can we ask
or have?

.................................................................................................

.................................................................................................

.................................................................................................

.................................................................................................

# Day 102

## *The Hope of Israel*

*O the hope of Israel, the saviour thereof in time of trouble,
why shouldest thou be as a stranger in the land, and as a wayfaring
man that turneth aside to tarry for a night?*

JEREMIAH 14:8

"The Hope of His People," Israel, is also the Hope of His Bride, the church. Israel will be regathered and become, though now despised of man and all nations, the foremost kingdom in all the earth. And He will come, too, and He will be both "Hope" and full fruition to every believing soul.

*"Even so come, Lord Jesus, come quickly."* Amen.

..................................................................................................................

..................................................................................................................

..................................................................................................................

..................................................................................................................

# Day 103

## A Righteous Branch

*Behold, the days come, saith the LORD, that I will raise unto David a righteous Branch, and a King shall reign and prosper, and shall execute judgment and justice in the earth.*

JEREMIAH 23:5

A "righteous servant" is one who serves righteously, satisfying every command of his master. A "righteous branch" is one which rightly respects, honors, and bears fruit to the tree from which it grows. "Ye are branches," our Savior said of us, but He also said, "My Father pruneth." He who is the Righteous Branch heard the Father say, "This is my beloved Son, in whom I am well pleased" (Matthew 3:17). Will we not seek with all our hearts to abide in Him that we will glorify the Father by bearing much fruit?

........................................................................................................................

........................................................................................................................

........................................................................................................................

........................................................................................................................

# Day 104

## *David, Their King*

*But they shall serve the LORD their God, and David their king,*
*whom I will raise up unto them.*
JEREMIAH 30:9

What doubt, what incredulity of men has blinded human eyes for fear
that they should see that David, Israel's King, will truly be raised up
before them! How much we lose of deep reality, of wondrous truth and
vivid picture in the Word of God because our eyes are held shut through
our unbelief. How beautiful, how wonderful, that Christ our coming
Lord should call Himself "David, Their King." What are our thoughts
and prayers concerning Israel? Are we seeking, hoping for their King and
telling them that He is our King, too? And praying that their eyes may
be anointed to see in Christ, "David, Their King"!

# Day 105

## Resting Place

*My people hath been lost sheep: their shepherds have caused them to go astray, they have turned them away on the mountains: they have gone from mountain to hill, they have forgotten their restingplace.*

JEREMIAH 50:6

Truly there is rest for the weary, for Jesus is "Our Resting Place." Therefore, in the middle of the toil and the weariness, in the middle of the struggle and strife, let us ask that our ears may be opened to hear Him who said, "Come unto me, all ye that labour and are heavy laden, and I will give you rest" (Matthew 11:28). To abide in Him in continuous love and obedient faith is to find Him "Our Resting Place."

...........................................................................................................................

...........................................................................................................................

...........................................................................................................................

...........................................................................................................................

# Day 106

## *The Shepherd of Israel*

*And I will set up one shepherd over them. . .
and he shall be their shepherd.*

EZEKIEL 34:23

Is any name of our God more comforting to weary, needy children
than Jesus' name of Shepherd? Feeding, leading beside still water,
watching over all our wanderings, bringing us as the Shepherd of
Israel brought His flock out of the wilderness over the Jordan into the
land of peace and plenty.

*Teach us to trust in You, O Shepherd of Israel. Amen.*

.......................................................................................................................................................

.......................................................................................................................................................

.......................................................................................................................................................

.......................................................................................................................................................

# Day 107

## *Feeder*

*And I will set up one shepherd over them,
and he shall feed them, even my servant David;
he shall feed them, and he shall be their shepherd.*

EZEKIEL 34:23

The lie of the devil to God's children is always that they are "lost." Or that "difficulty is a sign that God has ceased to know or care." When we have wandered from Him, from right, from rest, from peace, "He restoreth my soul." It is His self-appointed task—the work which love makes a necessity for Him, as well as for His wandering sheep.

> *How gentle God's commands,
> How kind His precepts are.*

*What* He feeds is as important for us to learn as *when* and *where*. So let us cultivate our appetite, our longing, for His righteousness, and we will find He is "Our Feeder."

......................................................................................................................

......................................................................................................................

......................................................................................................................

......................................................................................................................

# Day 108

## A Plant of Renown

*And I will raise up for them a plant of renown,
and they shall be no more consumed with hunger in the land,
neither bear the shame of the heathen any more.*

EZEKIEL 34:29

Although our Lord came as a tender plant, and with no form nor beauty, yet has He become a "Plant of Renown," for already no other name is so widely known, no other name carries such wondrous power, no other name shows such boundless grace, and sometime, perhaps soon, "every knee shall bow and every tongue pro-claim" that "the tender plant" is a "Plant of Renown," that "Jesus Christ is Lord, to the glory of God the Father."

.................................................................................................................

.................................................................................................................

.................................................................................................................

.................................................................................................................

# Day 109

## A Stone Cut without Hands

*Thou sawest till that a stone was cut out without hands,
which smote the image upon his feet that were of iron and clay,
and brake them to pieces. . .and the stone that smote the image
became a great mountain, and filled the whole earth.*

DANIEL 2:34–35

Men plan for peace in human governments, build courts of
arbitration, leagues of nations, pacts and pledges, only to find them
crumbling in utter failure before the human work is half complete.
The Eternal God is planning a kingdom and government that cannot
fail, and He the King, whose shape and form and size and power are
ordered by the Most High God, will wipe out in His coming every
man-made plan. Are we looking for that "Stone" to come and smite?
Will we be "ready in the day of His power"?

......................................................................................................................

......................................................................................................................

......................................................................................................................

......................................................................................................................

# Day 110

## *The Ancient of Days*

*I saw in the night visions, and, behold, one like the Son of man*
*came with the clouds of heaven, and came to the Ancient of days,*
*and they brought him near before him. . .His dominion is an*
*everlasting dominion, which shall not pass away,*
*and his kingdom that which shall not be destroyed.*

DANIEL 7:13–14

"In the beginning was the Word," and He who redeemed us is "The
Ancient of Days," whose head is white as snow (Revelation 1:14). He
was from everlasting and will be to the ages of ages our Eternal God.
Will not we, whose life on the earth is but a hand-breadth, bow in
worship and adoration at the feet of "The Ancient of Days"?

........................................................................................................

........................................................................................................

........................................................................................................

........................................................................................................

# Day 111

## The Prince of Princes

*He shall also stand up against the Prince of princes;*
*but he shall be broken without hand.*
### DANIEL 8:25

By every word which men could understand Almighty God has sought to exalt His Son, so that in all things He might have the preeminence in our lives, as King of kings, as Lord of lords, and as in this text, "The Prince of princes." In earthly kingdoms it is very often true that on the prince who is heir apparent to the throne is lavished more affection than on the king himself. What about our love and affection to "The Prince of princes"? Although sitting now at the right hand of the Father and one with Him, He is waiting to be crowned on earth. Do we pay Him more devotion and deeper love than we do to these erring mortals who reign over us? Let us, in the real things of daily life, exalt Him to His rightful place and pour out our devotion to Him.

.......................................................................................................................................

.......................................................................................................................................

.......................................................................................................................................

.......................................................................................................................................

# Day 112

## *The Hope of His People*

*The LORD also shall roar out of Zion, and utter his voice from Jerusalem;
and the heavens and the earth shall shake: but the LORD will be the hope
of his people, and the strength of the children of Israel.*
JOEL 3:16

There is no hope apart from Him; no hope in self to win against the
world, the flesh, and the devil! No hope in self to either be or do what
will bless the world; but there is glorious hope for those who trust in
Him. Jesus who is our Savior, King, and Bridegroom, the Living Head
of the Body of which we are but humble members, "He is the Hope of
His People." He it is that "worketh in me both to will and to do."

.................................................................................................................

.................................................................................................................

.................................................................................................................

.................................................................................................................

# Day 113

## Ruler

*But thou, Bethlehem Ephratah, though thou be little among the thousands of Judah, yet out of thee shall he come forth unto me that is to be ruler in Israel; whose goings forth have been from of old, from everlasting.*

MICAH 5:2

Never in the history of the world has there been such hopeless failure of human governments as now. Never such high ideals, and never have high ideals fallen so flat. Great plans are made and conferences held to promote peace and good government, and like flimsy houses of cards the highest hopes are shattered in ruthless, heartless, brutal war. So must it be until He who has the right to reign comes and is "Ruler," not alone in Israel, but in all the world. More than thirty years ago one who was a chosen spokesman of the Lord said, "Perhaps He would have come sooner if we had, from our hearts, prayed more earnestly 'Thy Kingdom come.' " Do we ask it and sincerely desire it?

.................................................................................................................

.................................................................................................................

.................................................................................................................

.................................................................................................................

# Day 114

## *Stronghold*

*The LORD is good, a strong hold in the day of trouble;
and he knoweth them that trust in him.*

NAHUM 1:7

During the late terrible war when the huge blimps sailed over London,
multitudes of people hid in the subways. In the highlands of Central
Africa there is a section known as "The Iron Stone Plateau," where the
amount of ore appears to attract the lightning, and many adventurers
in that section stopping long at a place dig cellars into which they go
when thunderstorms arise. There are dangerous storms which assault
our spiritual life from which there is no safe retreat but Christ. Is He
your "Stronghold"? Have you learned to hide in Him?

......................................................................................................

......................................................................................................

......................................................................................................

......................................................................................................

# Day 115

## *Wall of Fire*

*For I, saith the LORD, will be unto her a wall of fire round about,
and will be the glory in the midst of her.*

ZECHARIAH 2:5

All the defense that we need is God to those who trust in Him. A "Wall of Fire" through which the fiercest foe can never come. The foe of evil thoughts will be burned. The hasty tongue will be consumed. The selfish desire that creeps so insidiously through every other barricade will be consumed by Him who is a Wall of Fire when we hide in Him.

..............................................................................................................................

..............................................................................................................................

..............................................................................................................................

..............................................................................................................................

# Day 116

## *My Servant, the Branch*

*Hear now, O Joshua the high priest, thou, and thy fellows that sit before thee: for they are men wondered at: for, behold, I will bring forth my servant the BRANCH.*

ZECHARIAH 3:8

No lesson, not even that of courage, is more often repeated, and perhaps none is more often needed, than the lesson given to us in our Lord's humility. He upon whose shoulders the Father laid all government; He who is the Mighty God; He who, "even when he subsisted in the form of God," "made himself of no reputation" (Philippians 2:7) and became not only the Branch but "My Servant," and in doing this has marked the pathway for every child of God. Are you God's *servant*, serving Him as your only Master, doing joyfully and eagerly His will? If in anything you have sought to follow any other master, will you submit your life, your *all* to Him, and be His Servant now?

......................................................................................................

......................................................................................................

......................................................................................................

......................................................................................................

# Day 117
## King over All the Earth

*And his feet shall stand in that day upon the mount of Olives. . .*
*and the LORD my God shall come, and all the saints with thee. . . .*
*And the LORD shall be king over all the earth:*
*in that day shall there be one LORD, and his name one.*
ZECHARIAH 14:4–5, 9

Someday, God grant it may be soon, "His feet shall stand upon the mount of Olives," and all the earth shall know that He is King. Can any flight of swift imagination exceed that picture? Through all the strife of nations, all the pride and rivalry of kings, what peace, what glory, what undreamed of wonders will be seen when He, "The King of kings," reigns "over all the earth." Does that day not allure you? Does the Spirit-given cry not fill all your soul—"Even so, come, Lord Jesus" (Revelation 22:20).

.................................................................................................................................

.................................................................................................................................

.................................................................................................................................

.................................................................................................................................

# Day 118

## *The Branch*

*And speak unto him, saying, Thus speaketh the Lord of hosts, saying,
Behold the man whose name is The Branch; and he shall grow up out
of his place, and he shall build the temple of the Lord.*

ZECHARIAH 6:12

While He was here on earth "The Branch" said, "The Son can do
nothing of himself, but what he seeth the Father do" (John 5:19),
taking the place of humility in His utter dependence upon God the
Father. Are we tempted to exalt ourselves, to work in some strength
which He has given in the past? Let us bow at His feet and remember
that except "ye abide in me ye can do nothing." Let us consider Him
who, although He was the Mighty God, still called Himself in His
earthly relationship "The Branch."

.......................................................................................................

.......................................................................................................

.......................................................................................................

.......................................................................................................

# Day 119
## Jehovah My God

*And ye shall flee by the valley of my mountains. . .*
*and Jehovah my God shall come, and all the holy ones with thee.*
ZECHARIAH 14:5 ASV

The Self-existing One, seeking always to reveal Himself to His children and to the world that does not know Him, is pleased and glorified when that revelation leads our souls to cry "Jehovah, my God." If "that thing or person who most absorbs our thought is our God," then who is my God today? The matchless Jehovah? Or some other being or created thing, unworthy of my trust and worship? Let us not rest until from our inmost soul we cry, "Jehovah, my God."

.................................................................................................

.................................................................................................

.................................................................................................

.................................................................................................

# Day 120
## The King

*And it shall come to pass, that every one that is left of all the
nations which came against Jerusalem shall even go up from
year to year to worship the King, the LORD of hosts,
and to keep the feast of tabernacles.*
ZECHARIAH 14:16

He is King; it does not matter that earth refused to crown Him and to
acknowledge His right to reign. He only waits for the Father's day and
hour to receive the kingdom which is His. The world waits and weeps;
the whole creation groans in pain for lack of the conditions that will
be when men have crowned Him King. We join that grief, but have we
truly crowned Him in our lives? Does He reign supremely every day,
in every act, and rule our words and thoughts? There will be joy in His
heart, joy in heaven, and joy in your heart, when you fully and with no
reserve crown Jesus King and Lord of All.

......................................................................................................................................

......................................................................................................................................

......................................................................................................................................

......................................................................................................................................

# Day 124

## The Messenger of the Covenant

*Behold, I will send my messenger. . .
even the messenger of the covenant, whom ye delight in:
behold, he shall come, saith the LORD of hosts.*

MALACHI 3:1

He who is our example that we should walk in His steps has called Himself "The Messenger of the Covenant." The Father gave a promise to those who believe in His Son. The Son came bringing that promise, that covenant—a Messenger sent from heaven. To the true believer that most precious covenant is "I will put my laws into their hearts, and in their minds will I write them" (Hebrews 10:16). Will you accept it now? "Open thy mouth wide, and I will fill it" (Psalm 84:10).

...........................................................................................................................

...........................................................................................................................

...........................................................................................................................

...........................................................................................................................

# Day 122

## *Refiner*

*And he shall sit as a refiner and purifier of silver:*
*and he shall purify the sons of Levi, and purge them as gold and silver,*
*that they may offer unto the LORD an offering in righteousness.*
MALACHI 3:3

When grosser things which men can see are removed from our lives,
there is grave danger that we will be satisfied and forget that still as
the heaven is high above the earth, so high are His ways above our
ways and His thoughts above our thoughts. That there is a finer life,
a deeper, holier peace, a clearer, surer likeness of the Lord possible for
His children, needs to be understood. And though through all of life
we may seem to have been in the melting pot, will we not say to Him
again at any cost, "Dear Refiner, make me what You will. Refine me
by any process that seems good to You"?

.............................................................................................................................

.............................................................................................................................

.............................................................................................................................

.............................................................................................................................

# Day 123

## Purifier

*And he shall sit as a. . .purifier of silver.*
MALACHI 3:3

No work of God shows more plainly His boundless love than His desire to purify our lives. So much impurity is found in us that we need to be tried in the furnace of affliction and to be purged like gold and silver. The difficult experiences through which we pass may often be understood as the infinite love of the Father, seeking to separate the impure from our lives, to bring us to a point of purity where we may see and reflect His image.

.........................................................................................................................

.........................................................................................................................

.........................................................................................................................

.........................................................................................................................

# Day 124

## The Sun of Righteousness

*But unto you that fear my name shall the Sun of righteousness
arise with healing in his wings.*
MALACHI 4:2

Jesus said, "When the Spirit of truth is come he shall convince the
world of—righteousness—because I go to the Father." Among all the
sons of men "there is none righteous, no, not one" (Romans 3:10).
But He who worked in the creation of the worlds, and walked the
streets of Judea, sits at the "right hand of the Father" in glory. He is
the Sun whose radiant righteousness heals our sin-sick souls.

*Lord Jesus, we come with our earth stains and our innumerable
faults and infirmities and bow at Your feet and worship You
while we seek the "healing in Your wings."*

.................................................................................................

.................................................................................................

.................................................................................................

.................................................................................................

# Day 125
## Jesus Christ

*The book of the generation of Jesus Christ.*
MATTHEW 1:1

Here is the first title given to our Lord in the New Testament—Jesus Christ. Matthew 1 contains a host of names, covering three periods of fourteen generations each, but *one* Name stands out like a radiant star to light all the others; *one Person* to whom all must render allegiance—Jesus (Savior) Christ (the Anointed One). At His feet every knee will bow in heaven and on earth.

*Let us pour out our hearts to Him in praise and in prayer this day and every day. Amen.*

.................................................................................................................

.................................................................................................................

.................................................................................................................

.................................................................................................................

# Day 126
## The Son of David

*The book of the generation of Jesus Christ, the son of David.*
MATTHEW 1:1

Our Lord was a lineal descendant of David, the king. This entitled Him to the right of sovereignty over David's land, and when He was here among men, we are told, there was no other claimant to the throne of David. Herod sought to destroy the Child-King Jesus, but Egypt was chosen as a refuge place for Him. The heart of Herod was like the hearts of all the children of men who will not have Him to rule over them. He was bearing us on His heart, as a Child, for He is the same "yesterday, today, and forever," and He is our refuge now.

*Jesus Christ, Son of David, may our hearts be linked up with Your great heart always. Amen.*

........................................................................................................

........................................................................................................

........................................................................................................

........................................................................................................

# Day 127

## Son of Abraham

*The book of the generation of Jesus Christ. . .the son of Abraham.*
MATTHEW 1:1

Three titles in one verse, "Jesus Christ—Son of David—Son of Abraham." Abraham was the head of the covenant nation. God had given to him the promise that in his seed should all the nations of the earth be blessed. Jesus submitted to the Jewish law in righteousness. He lived as a Jew, and He preached to the Jews. He died for the Jews as well as for all people. "So then they which be of faith are blessed with faithful Abraham" (Galatians 3:9). How wonderful! God manifested in the flesh as Abraham's seed and yet the One who made the promise to Abraham!

*Oh promised Son of Abraham and Son of God, our Savior, hold us fast in faith in Your Word. Amen.*

..................................................................................................................

..................................................................................................................

..................................................................................................................

..................................................................................................................

# Day 128

## *Jesus*

*Thou shalt call his name JESUS:*
*for he shall save his people from their sins.*
MATTHEW 1:21

Over seven hundred times in the New Testament is this name used—"Jesus" (Joshua). How familiar we are with that name! Joshua of the Old Testament saved Israel by leading them through the River Jordan, fought their battles, and was steadfast in his allegiance to God and His people. He was a type of our Lord who is our Joshua; who fights our battles for us; who is our Leader, our Protector, our Savior! Who will never cease His lordship until He has us safely in the fold on the other side. Hallelujah, what a Savior!

*This day, Savior of our souls, in whom we are set apart for eternity,*
*guide us by Your Holy Spirit to the praise of Your grace. Amen.*

........................................................................................

........................................................................................

........................................................................................

........................................................................................

# Day 129

## *Emmanuel*

*Behold, a virgin. . .shall bring forth a son,*
*and they shall call his name Emmanuel.*
MATTHEW 1:23

This was the prophecy of Isaiah 7:14: "Therefore the Lord himself shall give you a sign; Behold, a virgin shall conceive, and bear a son, and shall call his name Immanuel." "Emmanuel" (God with us)! What a wonderful God and Savior He is, and He is with us as He promised in Matthew 28:19–20: "Go ye therefore, and teach all nations, baptizing them in the name of the Father, and of the Son, and of the Holy Ghost: Teaching them to observe all things whatsoever I have commanded you: and, lo, I am with you always, even unto the end of the world." Let us sense His presence and make Him real. Walk, talk, live with, and love Him more and more as the days go by.

*Lord Jesus, we know that You dwell in us.*
*May we enjoy Your fellowship today. Amen.*

.................................................................................................

.................................................................................................

.................................................................................................

.................................................................................................

# Day 130

## A Governor

*And thou Bethlehem. . .out of thee shall come a Governor,*
*that shall rule my people Israel.*
MATTHEW 2:6

Bethlehem of Judah! A little village, twice highly honored! The birthplace of David, king of Israel, and the birthplace of Jesus the Christ, King of kings and Lord of lords! Who could visit this Land of Promise and not desire to see this city of cities, the place where Jehovah enthroned in human form and lying in a manger gazed into the face of the Virgin Mary, His mother. The government will be on His shoulders, and He will reign in righteousness. Blessed day!

*We pray for its soon coming and ask*
*for grace that we may hurry it. Amen.*

.......................................................................................................................

.......................................................................................................................

.......................................................................................................................

.......................................................................................................................

# Day 131
## The Young Child

*When they had heard the king, they departed;*
*and, lo, the star, which they saw in the east, went before them,*
*till it came and stood over where the young child was.*

MATTHEW 2:9

A star in the East led the wise men to a Star that outshines all the stars of heaven. Look at this Young Child! Fix your gaze upon His face, lying there, His eyes looking into your own inquiring eyes. Visualize, if you can, God manifested in the flesh for you. God—the Young Child! The Creator of all things! Before whom are thirty years of human life in which He will toil with His fellow men. Mystery of mysteries!

*Oh wonderful One, as we bow before You today, help us to discern*
*something of Your devotion for the sons of men. Amen.*

.................................................................................................................

.................................................................................................................

.................................................................................................................

.................................................................................................................

# Day 132

## A Nazarene

*And he came and dwelt in a city called Nazareth:*
*that it might be fulfilled which was spoken by the prophets,*
*He shall be called a Nazarene.*

MATTHEW 2:23

Nazareth was a town in the northern border of the plain of Esdraelon.
Here came the angel Gabriel and announced to Mary the coming birth
of Christ: "And the angel came in unto her, and said, Hail, thou that
art highly favoured, the Lord is with thee: blessed art thou among
women" (Luke 1:28). On the night of His betrayal our Lord asked the
question, "Whom seek ye?" They replied, "Jesus of Nazareth," and
He said, "I am He" (see John 18:4–5).

*Jesus of Nazareth, may we never be ashamed to*
*be called the followers of the lowly Nazarene.*

.................................................................................................

.................................................................................................

.................................................................................................

.................................................................................................

# Day 133
## *Friend of Sinners*

*Behold. . .a friend of publicans and sinners.*
MATTHEW 11:19

These are the words of Jesus Himself. He quotes their own phrases as applied to Himself. What a title! How wonderfully true it is—"A Friend of Sinners!" So He was and so He is—a Friend that sticks closer than a brother. Laying aside the royal robes of heaven, he came here to befriend sinful men. It was a lifework that cost Him His life. Hallelujah! What a Friend! How gladly He paid the price of friendship. As we take up the work of the day, let us ask ourselves the question, "Am I a friend of sinners?" If not, then I am not like my Lord, for He was and He joyed in it.

*Lord Jesus, the world is full of friendless sinners. May we make them acquainted with You who are their Friend. Amen.*

.......................................................................................................

.......................................................................................................

.......................................................................................................

.......................................................................................................

# Day 134
## *The Servant of Jehovah*

*Behold my servant, whom I have chosen.*
MATTHEW 12:18

Jesus, the prophesied Servant! Isaiah had portrayed Him. Jehovah had chosen Him. All of God's ways were known to Him from the beginning. You hear the echo of His voice, "I delight to do thy will, O my God!" Nothing was too great for Him to do, for He was the Creator, and nothing was too hard for Him, for He had all power. Nothing was too small for Him to do, for He stooped to notice a widow's mite and give a mighty lesson from it. What a gracious privilege to be yoked with Him in service.

*Dear Lord, let us labor with You, the "Servant of Jehovah,"*
*today and thus make it a good day for You. Amen.*

.............................................................................................................

.............................................................................................................

.............................................................................................................

.............................................................................................................

# Day 135
## My Beloved

*Behold. . .my beloved, in whom my soul is well pleased.*
MATTHEW 12:18

Twenty-seven times in the Song of Solomon is this title used for our Lord. God's Son was a *beloved* Servant. How dear He was to the Father—dear as the apple of His eye. Yet His love for us was manifest in the surrender of His Son to pay the penalty of our sin. "Greater love hath no man than this" (John 15:13). "While we were yet sinners, Christ died for us" (Romans 5:8). In the hour of darkness He cried, "My God, my God, why hast thou forsaken me?" (Mark 15:34). The agony, the grief, the pain He suffered, all had a voice which rings out the message "God so loved."

*Our Father, Your love for us has broken all the barriers down;*
*and we pray that Your Spirit may rest upon us this day as*
*we meditate upon the greatness of Your love. Amen.*

.......................................................................................................

.......................................................................................................

.......................................................................................................

.......................................................................................................

# Day 136

## A Sower

*He that soweth the good seed is the Son of man.*
MATTHEW 13:37

The seed is the Word of God. God's Son sowed the good seed. He soweth the Word of Truth in the hearts of men. When we sow the Gospel we sow good seed. When we give out the Word of God we are sowing good seed. Nothing is comparable to the *Word* itself. It has potential power. It is a *living* seed and never fails. We are to imitate our Lord, the Sower, and see that the pure seed of the Word is scattered wherever we go. "Sow beside all waters" (Isaiah 32:20).

*Lord, make me a seed sower today, and hear my prayer for all the sowers in all the world. Amen!*

.................................................................................

.................................................................................

.................................................................................

.................................................................................

# Day 137
## *The Christ*

*Thou art the Christ, the Son of the living God.*
MATTHEW 16:16

This is the title of the long-looked-for Savior—the Anointed One.
Prophets had foretold His coming and now His kingly authority
is recorded. Over three hundred times is this title used in the New
Testament. From "Christ" comes the word "Christian," and from
"Christian" comes the word "Christianity." Today this land of ours is
the foremost Christian nation of the world. Our gospel is the Gospel
of Christ of which we are not ashamed, for it is the power of God
unto salvation to everyone that believes.

*Lord, as "Christ-ones" let us honor You by having the same anointing
power resting on us as we enter the service of the day. Amen.*

.............................................................................................................................

.............................................................................................................................

.............................................................................................................................

.............................................................................................................................

# Day 138

## *Jesus the Christ*

*Then charged he his disciples that they should tell no man
that he was Jesus the Christ.*

MATTHEW 16:20

This title, "Jesus the Christ," is used a hundred times in the New
Testament. "The Savior—the Anointed One"—a combination that
magnifies the office of the One whom we long to worship. The time
had not yet come for them to preach the story of redemption. They
were to hold their peace for a season, but He tells *us* to go into all the
world and tell to all people the wonderful message of Jesus Christ and
His finished work. Are we obeying the command?

*Dear Father, as we go out today with this precious Name
in our hearts and on our lips, help us to tell someone of the
wonders of the Man, Your Son, Jesus the Christ! Amen.*

.......................................................................................................................

.......................................................................................................................

.......................................................................................................................

.......................................................................................................................

# Day 139
## My Beloved Son

*This is my beloved Son, in whom I am well pleased; hear ye him.*
MATTHEW 17:5

Wonderful manifestation! A cloud of glory overshadowing what was too deep for human eyes to penetrate. The voice of Jehovah attesting that Jesus was His beloved Son and that His words were to be heard. The same voice and the same message were heard in chapter 3, verse 17 when our Lord was baptized, and once again in John 12:28 in Jerusalem. "*His* beloved" and *our* beloved! How marvelous is that testimony to Him whom we have learned to love, and because we love Him, we are beloved of the Father.

*Lord, may we breathe it over and over again today,*
*"I am my beloved's and my beloved is mine." Amen.*

........................................................................................................................

........................................................................................................................

........................................................................................................................

........................................................................................................................

# Day 140

## The Prophet of Nazareth

*This is Jesus the prophet of Nazareth of Galilee.*
MATTHEW 21:11

This great demonstration had been planned by God and foretold by Him (Zechariah 9:9). Our Lord comes into Jerusalem riding upon the foal of a donkey. The crowd is vast; the enthusiasm is great. "Who is this?" is the cry; and the answer is, "This is Jesus, The Prophet of Nazareth." A despised Nazarene! A prophet from an obscure village! We are all proud if, by chance, we were born in some noted place; but God, when He took the form of a man, was born in a manger and made His home in Nazareth. For our sakes He became poor, that we through His poverty might be made rich.

*Let us meditate on the riches of His grace, bow at His feet and kiss them as we adore Him; and may we walk humbly today with the despised Nazarene. Amen.*

.......................................................................................................

.......................................................................................................

.......................................................................................................

.......................................................................................................

# Day 141
## *Master*

*One is your Master, even Christ; and all ye are brethren.*
MATTHEW 23:8

"Master" here means "Teacher," or some say, "Leader." The admonition is to avoid the desire for personal distinction so common among God's leaders. Let our eyes be fixed on Him and depend on the Holy Spirit who represents Him and who guides us into *all* truth (John 16:13–14). The more we seek to exalt Him, the less will we think of magnifying ourselves. Make Him Master of your life today, remembering that "The disciple is not above his master: but every one that is perfect shall be as his master" (Luke 6:40).

*Oh, that we may be like our Master, the meek and lowly One! For today, our Lord, we need great grace as we seek to follow You as Master. Amen.*

......................................................................................................................

......................................................................................................................

......................................................................................................................

......................................................................................................................

# Day 142
## The Bridegroom

*And while they went to buy, the bridegroom came.*
MATTHEW 25:10

The Bridegroom must come. The true church is His beloved espoused bride. He has waited a long, long time for her to prepare herself for the glad day and to add the last one which will complete the body. Are you thinking of Him today as the Coming One? And of yourself as one of those who are to be blessed as His beloved throughout eternity? How insignificant are all the little cares and trials! How small they seem when our eyes are turned with expectancy toward Him as He comes in the clouds. "Blessed are they which are called unto the marriage supper of the Lamb" (Revelation 19:9). Hallelujah!

*May our prayer always be, "Even so, come, Lord Jesus, come quickly." Amen.*

..........................................................................................................................

..........................................................................................................................

..........................................................................................................................

..........................................................................................................................

# Day 143
## *The Holy One of God*

*I know thee who thou art, the Holy One of God.*
MARK 1:24

What a testimony coming from the lips of one possessed of an unclean spirit, Satan's tool, under his power. But the presence of Christ subdued him. "I know thee who thou art, the Holy One of God." This was not a willing testimony but was forced from him. Many men are devil-possessed, and the devil has powers accorded him, but Christ can hinder his followers, can cast out his demons and forbid their speaking (verse 34). How lovingly we should bow at His feet—the Holy One of God! May we fix our thoughts on Him and say many times today as we walk and talk with Him,

*"Oh Thou Holy One of God, glorify Yourself through us." Amen.*

.............................................................................................

.............................................................................................

.............................................................................................

.............................................................................................

# Day 144
## *Our Brother*

*For whosoever shall do the will of God, the same is my brother.*
MARK 3:35

If this is true, and it is, then the reverse is also true, and He is our Brother. The picture is given in the thirty-first and thirty-fourth verses: "There came then his brethren and his mother, and, standing without, sent unto him, calling him. . . . And he looked round about on them which sat about him, and said, Behold my mother and my brethren!" How wonderful that He should graciously give this title to those who do the Father's will! And what is that will? The acceptance of His Son as our Savior and Lord, and the submission of our will to His will as revealed in His Word, for His Word is His will. How near and dear He is to us, our Lord and our Brother! Fix it in your thoughts—"Ours by faith; ours forever."

*Dear Lord, keep us in loving fellowship with Yourself today. Amen.*

# Day 145
## Thou Son of the Most High God

*And cried with a loud voice, and said, What have I to do with thee,*
*Jesus, thou Son of the most high God?*
MARK 5:7

Here we are confronted with another testimony from an unclean
spirit—"Son of the most high God," he calls Jesus. What unseen
powers compelled this significant title? Was it brought about by being
face-to-face with Himself? Judas betrayed Him, but this poor, demon-
possessed man worshipped Him. In these strange days many teachers,
professors, and preachers refuse to honor Him as *the Son*, but only as
*a Son* of God. But we lift our hearts to Him and say,

> *"Son of the most high God, be our companion this day*
> *and may we withhold nothing from You."* Amen.

.........................................................................................................................

.........................................................................................................................

.........................................................................................................................

.........................................................................................................................

# Day 146
## *The Carpenter*

*Is not this the carpenter?*
MARK 6:3

The Carpenter! Two things are suggested in this verse. Joseph is not mentioned and is probably not living. Jesus is working at the carpenter's bench and continued to do so until He assumed His place in His public ministry. We can and should visualize Him in His daily tasks—a man among men. How near He seems to us! What a joy to know that He handled the hammer and sharpened the saw, planed the plank, and helped to supply the food for the family. Test this picture of Him with any false system and observe the contrast. No matter what our calling may be, the Carpenter will be one with us. We can walk arm in arm with Him in our daily tasks.

*O, Carpenter of Galilee, be our ideal always! Amen.*

..................................................................................................................................................

..................................................................................................................................................

..................................................................................................................................................

..................................................................................................................................................

# Day 147
## The Son of Mary

*Is not this. . .the son of Mary?*
MARK 6:3

The Carpenter, the "Son of Mary," has come back to His hometown from an evangelistic trip in which He had worked many miracles. The people were astonished at His teaching. Prejudice possessed them. "Is not this the Son of Mary?" We never worship Mary as our Catholic friends do, but we do honor her above all women—God's chosen vessel to bear His Son and fulfill His prophecy. How true He was to the last. See Him on the cross and hear His last words to Mary, from John 19:26, "Woman, behold thy son" (John, the beloved, to whom He had said, "Behold thy mother").

*Blessed title–Son of Mary! The Babe who is one day to rule the world and at whose feet we will bow in worshipful adoration! Let us do so now. Amen.*

# Day 148
## Good Master

*Good Master, what shall I do that I may inherit eternal life?*
MARK 10:17

This question was asked of our Lord by a young man with great possessions, as recorded in Matthew 19:16. This is the concrete question of the soul of man, "What shall I *do* to secure a right to heaven?" The theme of *religion* is *do*; but the theme of our Lord was just the opposite, "Follow Me." Eternal life is a gift. Those who accept and follow Him find that He *is* the "Good Master" because He is the "God-Master," for only One is good and He is God, and He has provided for us a salvation—simple to accept but costing Him a price which involved His own life. How gracious is our God and how we should love and adore Him!

*Lord, may we walk in the sunshine of Your love today. Amen.*

.................................................................................

.................................................................................

.................................................................................

.................................................................................

# Day 149
## *Son of Man*

*The Son of man shall be delivered unto the chief priests,*
*and unto the scribes; and they shall condemn him to death.*
MARK 10:33

In the ninth chapter Jesus had said, "The Son of man is delivered into the hands of men and they shall kill him." How earnestly He sought to stress the fact of His approaching sacrifice upon His disciples and how He longed for their sympathy; but, alas, how hard is the human heart! How difficult it is for Him to win us to Himself! "The Son of man must suffer many things" (Mark 8:31), He had said, but the saddest of all was the failure of His own beloved disciples to enter into the burden He bore as He approached the cross.

*Oh Holy Son of Man, give to us the loving hearts that will*
*enter into fellowship with You in all things. Amen.*

.................................................................................

.................................................................................

.................................................................................

.................................................................................

# Day 150
## A Ransom

*The Son of man came. . .to give his life a ransom for many.*
MARK 10:45

"A Ransom for many!" Here Christ is identified as the penalty paid
for the sins of the world. As sinners under the judgment wrath of
God, He took our place and paid the penalty and the price of our
deliverance with His own blood. Listen to the drops of blood as they
fall from hands and feet and wounded side! They voice the words,
"The ransom price for *my* sins and for the sins of the whole world."
Oh, that men everywhere would believe it and receive it! How dear,
how precious is He to us, washed clean in His blood and freed forever
from the punishment due to us.

*Lord, may our ransomed souls well up in praise to*
*Your glorious Name! Amen.*

.......................................................................................................................

.......................................................................................................................

.......................................................................................................................

.......................................................................................................................

# Day 154

## One Son, His Well-Beloved

*Having yet therefore one son, his wellbeloved, he sent him
also last unto them, saying, They will reverence my son.*
MARK 12:6

The Savior is in Jerusalem. The chief priests and scribes come to Him
and question His authority. Jesus answers them in the parable of the
vineyard, picturing to them the treatment of the servants who were
sent to gather the fruit, telling the story—so old, so strange—of the
attitude of the human heart toward God. He sent His Son, His well-
beloved Son, and they took Him and killed Him and cast Him out.
How could they? They have cast Him out of the schools and many of
the churches, though all we have of earthly civilization and comforts
today we owe to Him.

*God's Well-beloved Son, we enthrone You today in our hearts.
Help us to worship and adore You. Amen.*

........................................................................................................

........................................................................................................

........................................................................................................

........................................................................................................

# Day 152

## Christ, the Son of the Blessed

*Art thou the Christ, the Son of the Blessed?*
MARK 14:61

The court is convened. The high priest is presiding. Charges had been brought against the Lord Jesus Christ by false witnesses, but they had not agreed. The high priest put to Him a question: "Art thou the Christ, the Son of the Blessed?" And He answered, "I am." There was no denial of the title, but a straight confession of His Sonship, Heirship, Power, and coming Glory. And when He comes—if He delays still a season—we will be among those who will be caught up in the clouds to meet Him in the air and with the hosts of heaven praise Him "Blessed!"

*Lord, Jesus Christ, Son of the Blessed, hurry the glad day. Amen.*

.................................................................................................................................

.................................................................................................................................

.................................................................................................................................

.................................................................................................................................

# Day 153
## The King of the Jews

*And Pilate asked him, Art thou the King of the Jews?*
*And he answering said unto them, Thou sayest it.*
MARK 15:2

What a title for our Lord to put His seal on at the time when the Jews were in subjection to the Romans and He Himself a prisoner before a judge. But He *is* King of the Jews—yes, *King of kings and Lord of all*. Pilate will yet stand before Him to be judged, and the Jewish people will yet proclaim Him as their own King. He is the Ruler. Let us give Him His rightful place as Ruler in our lives. How can we serve Him today? Perhaps in some definite prayer for the Jewish people and some testimony to them of the joy there is in knowing, loving, and serving Him.

*Lord, remember Your ancient people and all*
*who seek to make You known to them. Amen.*

# Day 154
## *The Son of the Highest*

*He shall be great, and shall be called the Son of the Highest.*
LUKE 1:32

This is the message of the angel to Mary, and here is a remarkable coincidence. In Mark 5:7, we have the evil spirit in the man in the tombs giving a similar title to Jesus, "Son of the most high God." The title given Him here is in fulfillment of Psalm 132:11: "The LORD hath sworn in truth unto David; he will not turn from it; of the fruit of thy body will I set upon thy throne." David's heir is to reign as Son of the Most High God, and that time only waits for the completion of the church which is His Body. Let us do our best each day to win souls for Him and thus hurry the day when we will be with Him and reign with Him.

*Son of the Highest, we bow to You, we worship You.*
*Help us to magnify Your name today. Amen.*

........................................................................

........................................................................

........................................................................

........................................................................

# Day 155
## *God My Savior*

*And my spirit hath rejoiced in God my Saviour.*
LUKE 1:47

The word *Savior* here is *Soter* meaning "presence." Should we not imitate Mary, the blessed woman, in magnifying our Savior and rejoicing in the finished work which He has produced in our behalf? It is never what *we* are but what *He* is. Our joy is in Him, and we rejoice with joy unspeakable and full of glory as we face today with joyful hearts. Will we not have a tender heart for those who do not know Him?

*Savior, like a shepherd lead us today to glorify Your*
*name in our efforts to win souls for You. Amen.*

.................................................................................................................

.................................................................................................................

.................................................................................................................

.................................................................................................................

# Day 156

## *Horn of Salvation*

*And hath raised up an horn of salvation for us
in the house of his servant David.*
LUKE 1:69

Here is a title which suggests the strength and power of our Lord—
"Horn of Salvation." The word *horn* as used in the scripture signifies
"strength" and is often found in Hebrew literature. In the horns, the
bull manifests his strength. The Lord Jesus Christ is our Strength and
a very present help in time of trouble (Psalms 118:14; 28:7; 37:39).
"But the salvation of the righteous is of the LORD: he is their strength
in the time of trouble" (Psalm 37:39). You may be tempted and tried
today. You may have burdens to bear. Let Him be your "Horn of
Salvation."

*Lord, strengthen us by the power of Your might
for today's service for You. Amen.*

# Day 157
## *The Highest*

*And thou, child, shalt be called the prophet of the Highest.*
LUKE 1:76

Listen to the voice of Zacharias, father of John the Baptist, as he voices the wonderful prophecy concerning his son who was to be the prophet of the Lord to prepare the way before Him. Our Lord is here named "The Highest," or better, "The Most High." He came from the heights of glory to be born in a manger. "Prophet" in the New Testament means "a public expounder," and to us, His redeemed ones, has been committed this honorable title. We are the expounders of this great revelation of the Bible concerning our most highly exalted Lord.

*Glory to God in the Highest, King of kings and Lord of lords, whom we claim as our own. Amen.*

.................................................................................

.................................................................................

.................................................................................

.................................................................................

# Day 158

## The Dayspring from on High

*Through the tender mercy of our God;*
*whereby the dayspring from on high hath visited us.*
LUKE 1:78

Zacharias is inspired as his soul goes out to speak of the coming of the Messiah. It has been suggested that the glory of the sunrise was breaking over the hills surrounding Jerusalem, and the golden glory lit up the horizon as his lips breathed the words inspired by the Spirit of God, "Dayspring from on High!" Perhaps the morning glory brought to the mind of Zacharias the message of Isaiah, "Arise, shine; for thy light is come, and the glory of the LORD is risen upon thee" (Isaiah 60:1).

*Before we take up our daily tasks, let us turn our eyes to the heavens*
*with grateful hearts and let the Holy Spirit flood our souls with the*
*glory of the risen, coming Christ. Amen.*

# Day 159

## Christ, the Lord

*For unto you is born this day in the city of David a Saviour,*
*which is Christ the Lord.*

LUKE 2:11

The heavens are opened now, and the message of the angel of the
Lord is announced—"good tidings of great joy." The message was
to the humble shepherds, and it will mean much to us if we can, in
humility of heart, take our place with the shepherds, acknowledge our
unworthiness, and take hold of the truth in our own souls—"Unto
you is born a Saviour, which is Christ the Lord" (the Anointed One—
the Ruler). We are no longer to rule ourselves. He is to rule us.

*Lord, with joy we submit our wills and surrender all to You.*
*Help us to magnify You this day. Amen.*

........................................................................................................................

........................................................................................................................

........................................................................................................................

........................................................................................................................

# Day 160
## *The Babe*

*Ye shall find the babe wrapped in swaddling clothes,*
*lying in a manger.*
LUKE 2:12

Again the voice of the angel rings out to the shepherds: "Christ the Lord—The Babe—lying in a manger." How easy it would be for the shepherds to find Him. No other newly born babe would be found "lying in a manger"—just One—and He, the altogether lovely One, the foremost among ten thousand! Sometimes the saints magnify their human birthright and place of birth, but He was to be a blessing to the humblest. Would not the cattle—could they have sensed the significance of the event—have bent their knees in homage to the Babe? How sad to know that millions in our land have not yet bowed their knees to Him.

*Lord, may we who have named Your name bow in humblest*
*submission to You today and pour out our hearts in joyful*
*praise to You, Babe of Bethlehem. Amen.*

.................................................................................................

.................................................................................................

.................................................................................................

.................................................................................................

# Day 164

## The Consolation of Israel

*There was a man in Jerusalem, whose name was Simeon;*
*and the same man was just and devout,*
*waiting for the consolation of Israel.*

LUKE 2:25

Simeon was just and devout and waited for the "Consolation of Israel." "Consolation" means "paraclete" (one coming alongside) as we think and speak of the Holy Spirit who comes to abide in and lead us out in our daily life. Simeon was waiting for the deliverance of the Jews by the coming of the Messiah. They did not as a nation receive Him, but some did and were consoled, and Israel will yet have the promised consolation, as Paul was comforted by the power of the indwelling Holy Spirit (1 Thessalonians 1:5).

*Lord, may we also rely upon the abiding comfort of the*
*indwelling of the Holy Spirit all the day. Amen.*

.....................................................................................................

.....................................................................................................

.....................................................................................................

.....................................................................................................

# Day 162

## The Lord's Christ

*And it was revealed unto him by the Holy Ghost, that he should not see death, before he had seen the Lord's Christ.*

LUKE 2:26

Simeon was a just and devout man who believed the Word of God and rested on its promises. The Holy Ghost came to him and made a revelation. He was not to taste of death until he had tasted the sweets of seeing and knowing "The Lord's Christ." The Lord never fails His loved ones. When He can get hold of the hearts of men and women, He is glad to make a revelation of Himself to them and give to them the power of the Holy Spirit. His great heart beats in sympathy with every pulsing of every loyal-hearted follower.

*Holy Spirit, give us new spiritual visions of the Lord's Christ. Amen.*

.........................................................................................

.........................................................................................

.........................................................................................

.........................................................................................

# Day 163
## *The Salvation of God*

*For mine eyes have seen thy salvation.*
LUKE 2:30

The aged saint Simeon, standing in the temple, took the child Jesus in his arms and, looking into His face, lifted his eyes to heaven and said: "Lord, now lettest thou thy servant depart in peace, according to thy word; for mine eyes have seen thy salvation." Long had he waited, long had he prayed, long had he desired to see Him. Now the Spirit of God reveals to him the fact that his heart's desire had been granted and that he was gazing on the Divine Savior of souls and death had no more terrors for him. There is only one cure for the world's unrest, "The Salvation of God." Let us go out today and tell the story wherever we can. The poor, hungry-hearted, sin-sick souls are waiting.

*Lord, guide us in this service to Your Glory. Amen.*

.................................................................................................

.................................................................................................

.................................................................................................

.................................................................................................

# Day 164

## A Light to Lighten the Gentiles

*A light to lighten the Gentiles, and the glory of thy people Israel.*
LUKE 2:32

The world has been a dark world ever since Adam and Eve listened to the temptation of Satan. There was no hope until God said: "The seed of the woman shall bruise the serpent's head"—a promise of coming victory for a lost race. He who is the light of the Gentiles is the light of the world (Matthew 4:16). The light shone for Israel first, but Israel rejected its blessed beams. But again the Light will shine for the people now wandering over the earth in darkness. What is the duty of believers? Is it not to lift the Light high so that the world of sinners in darkness may come into fellowship with Him?

*Lord of Light, help us to shine as lights in a dark world today. Amen.*

# Day 165

## *The Glory of Thy People Israel*

*A light to lighten the Gentiles, and the glory of thy people Israel.*
LUKE 2:32

The message of Paul was "to the Jew first," but here the Gentiles are mentioned first. The Jews turned away from Jesus and would not have Him to rule over them, but the Gentiles will not receive Him, either—just a few. The glory will rest on Israel when He comes with scepter in hand to rule a reconstructed earth. The Shekinah glory, manifested in the tabernacle and temple, will shine again on His beloved people and Jesus—the Jew—will be the glory of Israel in that day. Let us love the Jews and seek to bring the Gospel of the grace of God to them.

*Lord Jesus, who is the Glory of Thy People Israel, remember Your persecuted, penalty-paying people and help us to love them. Amen.*

......................................................................................................

......................................................................................................

......................................................................................................

......................................................................................................

# Day 166

## A Sign

*This child is set. . .for a sign which shall be spoken against.*
LUKE 2:34

Our Lord Jesus Christ was a significant sign to Israel. The prophecies had long before made clear that Israel was to be tested when the Messiah came. Some would believe and follow Him. Some would reject and crucify Him. Our Lord gave testimony to this fact when Pilate asked Him, "Art thou a King?" And His answer was: "To this end was I born, and for this cause came I into the world" (John 18:37). Poor Pilate, he had his evidence but would not accept it. Where is he? The Sign has been given to our land, also. Where are the multitudes? The same old story will be told again and again.

*Oh Lord, have compassion upon this poor land. Inspire Your servants to be brave and true in sounding the alarm. Amen.*

........................................................................................................

........................................................................................................

........................................................................................................

........................................................................................................

# Day 167
## The Child Jesus

*The child Jesus tarried behind in Jerusalem.*
LUKE 2:43

Here we have our first view of Jesus as a young boy, interested in the business of His heavenly Father. Hear Him when Joseph and Mary seek Him: "Wist ye not that I must be about my Father's business?" (Luke 2:49) The strangeness of the story of His life is a constant surprise. God manifested in the flesh—a Child—with words of wisdom falling from His lips—a message for us all, "Occupy (do business) till I come." Every disciple is a businessman or woman, and our business is the most important in all the world. Let us take as a motto for our daily life the words of the Child Jesus, "I must be about my Father's business."

*Lord, help us to be busy about Your business today. Amen.*

...................................................................................................................

...................................................................................................................

...................................................................................................................

...................................................................................................................

# Day 168

## *Physician*

*And he said unto them, Ye will surely say unto me this proverb,*
*Physician, heal thyself.*
LUKE 4:23

Our Lord had been in Galilee. His fame had spread throughout
that region. He had worked mighty miracles. He comes back home
to Nazareth where He had been brought up and preaches in the
synagogue on the Sabbath Day from Isaiah 61:1–3, saying, "This day
is this scripture fulfilled in your ears." The people who heard these
words said, "Is not this Joseph's son?" and then Jesus quoted to
them our verse, a proverb among the Jews. What a mistake they made.
He *was* the great Physician. He *is* the great Physician—"Able to do
exceeding abundantly above all that we ask or think" (Ephesians 3:20).
How few know Him as such a One! How few look to Him! How few
depend on Him!

*Lord who is the great Physician,*
*we look to You today to supply our every need. Amen.*

# Day 169

## *Lord of the Sabbath*

*And he said unto them, That the Son of man
is Lord also of the sabbath.*
LUKE 6:5

He is the Master (Lord) of the Sabbath. He is the Maker of heaven and earth. "Without him was not any thing made that was made." He is either what He claimed to be, or else He is the greatest impostor that ever lived. The Sabbath was made for man, and not man for the Sabbath. It is lawful to do good on the Sabbath. Serving others is serving the Lord of the Sabbath. He, with His disciples, picked and ate the wheat on the Sabbath, and on the Sabbath He healed the man with the withered hand. The Sabbath is the Lord's Day. Solve all your problems in connection with the Sabbath Day by the question, "What would the Lord do on this day?" Then whatever you do, whether you eat or drink, do all to the glory of God.

*Lord Jesus, we pray that every day may be a
good day for You through our lives. Amen.*

# Day 170

## A Great Prophet

*And they glorified God, saying, That a great prophet is risen up among us; and, That God hath visited his people.*

LUKE 7:16

Four centuries had elapsed since Malachi had passed away, and Israel had been without a prophetic voice. Now they are stirred by the presence of Jesus and glorify God. Israel was not forsaken. God's Word was true. And Jesus was a great Prophet; yes, greater even than they knew. Humble, quiet, gentle, no pomp, no display, but wonderful in works. Do *we* recognize His greatness? Do we believe His prophecies and promises? Do we possess them and profit by them and give glory to His name?

*Lord, help us to believe every word of the Prophetic Book. Amen.*

.................................................................................................

.................................................................................................

.................................................................................................

.................................................................................................

# Day 171

## The Christ of God

*He said unto them, But whom say ye that I am?*
*Peter answering said, The Christ of God.*
LUKE 9:20

Jesus was alone in prayer and asked His disciples the question,
"Whom say the people that I am?" and after they had given their
answers, He asked the question in our text. The disciples were
compelled to recognize His heavenly gifts, His greatness, His power,
and His gracious Spirit; but it was hard for them to think of Him as
One who must suffer persecution and death at the hands of the Jews.
But He knew all that was before Him and walked steadily on toward
the cruel cross on which He must die. Today the *professing* church is
inclined to reject the theme of His atoning blood, but those of us to
whom He is "the Christ of God" adore Him more and more as the
depths of His sacrifice and suffering are revealed.

*Lord, may we hold You in our hearts today as*
*"the Christ of God." Amen.*

........................................................................................................................

........................................................................................................................

........................................................................................................................

........................................................................................................................

# Day 172
## A Certain Samaritan

*But a certain Samaritan, as he journeyed. . .*
*had compassion on him.*
LUKE 10:33

The story of the Good Samaritan is familiar to all of us, but read it again. Here we take the liberty of viewing our Lord as "a certain Samaritan." Humanity was His neighbor. He loved all, lived for all, labored for all, and laid down His life for all. Being what He was and is, He could be nothing less, and we look up to Him today and glory in the mightiness of His humanity and the magnificence of His heart. If we are indeed Spirit-born, then there must be something of His loving-kindness in us, and the world is waiting for our touch. Let us take the Good Samaritan for our model today and pray,

*"Lord Jesus, make us more like Yourself."* Amen.

.................................................................................................................

.................................................................................................................

.................................................................................................................

.................................................................................................................

# Day 173
## The Master of the House

*When once the master of the house is risen up. . .*
*he shall answer and say unto you, I know you not whence ye are.*
LUKE 13:25

Here is a new title for our Lord—"Master of the House." How appropriate it is—"Lord of the house—the Head—the Governor." The "house" is heaven where He is to rule. The appeal is for earnest effort on the part of believers to impress upon the unsaved the fact that there is a heaven and there is a hell, and only *one gate* to heaven— Jesus Christ. Why do we not make more definite to people the awful consequences of failure to hear His voice *now* and that there will come a time when it will be too late?

*Dear Lord, may we labor and pray earnestly today that we may be faithful in urging upon people the necessity of decision for Christ. Amen.*

.............................................................................................................

.............................................................................................................

.............................................................................................................

.............................................................................................................

# Day 174

## A Guest

*And when they saw it, they all murmured, saying,*
*That he was gone to be guest with a man that is a sinner.*
LUKE 19:7

Zacchaeus was highly honored when Christ invited Himself to be his guest. How like our Lord! He knew Zacchaeus wanted to see Him, and He sought him out and became his guest. How we would congratulate ourselves were some noted person to come to our house to dine. What a fuss we would make. How we would boast about it. Why do we not tell the story to everybody "A Great One has come to live in my house?" "Who is He?" "He is the King of glory. He holds the worlds in the hollow of His hand. He lives with me."

*Oh blessed Guest, help us today to magnify*
*and glorify You before all. Amen.*

# Day 175
## A Certain Nobleman

*He said therefore, A certain nobleman went into a far country to receive for himself a kingdom, and to return.*
LUKE 19:12

The setting of this picture is remarkable. Our Lord is standing with the Jews around Him in the shadow of a palace built by a nobleman, Archelaus, who had gone to Rome and received the kingdom from Caesar. Our Lord is the Nobleman whose face was turned toward the land beyond the skies where He has gone and from where He will one day return. "Occupy till I come" is His message. He has entrusted to us, as His servants, the most valuable treasures of heaven—time, opportunity, the gifts of the Holy Spirit, a great wide world in which to transact the greatest of all business! Precious privileges are ours and a solemn account must be given.

*Lord, give us sharpness of vision to see and wisdom to utilize our opportunities in the investment of our lives for You. Amen.*

.............................................................................................

.............................................................................................

.............................................................................................

.............................................................................................

# Day 176
## *The Chosen of God*

*Let him save himself, if he be Christ, the chosen of God.*
LUKE 23:35

Christ is on the cross. He prays, "Father, forgive them." The people stand observing Him; the rulers deride Him and mock Him. What a picture! What a slur! "*If* thou be the Christ, the chosen of God." So do men today. The question mark grows as the days go by, but the title which was given Him in derision is a wonderfully true one and is found again in 1 Peter 2:4. Yes, indeed! Chosen before the foundation of the earth, and the *only One* who could be chosen for the great work of our redemption.

*Lord, You have chosen* Him, *and You have chosen* us.
*May we adore and glory in You today. Amen.*

.......................................................................................................

.......................................................................................................

.......................................................................................................

.......................................................................................................

# Day 177
## A Prophet Mighty in Deed and Word

*And he said unto them, What things? And they said unto him,*
*Concerning Jesus of Nazareth, which was a prophet mighty*
*in deed and word before God and all the people.*

LUKE 24:19

Some hated Him. Some worshipped Him. Mighty in life, mighty in death, and mighty in His resurrection! The rulers thought they had eliminated Him. Some seek to do so today. They crucified Him in fulfillment of scripture, but He is alive today. He lives in the hearts of millions who would be willing to be crucified for Him. He will live throughout the eternal ages, and every word He ever uttered will be fulfilled to the letter.

*O mighty Prophet, help us to lay hold of the Word with*
*intensified faith and hold fast until You return. Amen.*

.................................................................................................

.................................................................................................

.................................................................................................

.................................................................................................

# Day 178
## The Word

*In the beginning was the Word, and the Word was with God,
and the Word was God.*

JOHN 1:1

We come today to John's Gospel in which we will find many titles for
the Son of God. Here we confront the first—"The Word." The book
of Genesis commences with creation, but John commences with the
Creator. Behind all things with which we ever have had or will have
to do is the Word. "The Word was God!" What a foundation for our
faith when we know that Jesus was the Word and the Word was God.
Every day we can, if we will, be facing this tremendous fact, and as
we feel the throb of our heart, there is a voice that says, "God!" As we
look upon the heavens and the clouds—"God!" The sun, the moon,
the trees, the flowers, the living creatures, all are saying, "God!"
Without Him—nothing! With Him—all things!

*Oh Living Word, who have given us the written Word,
help us to abide in You today. Amen.*

........................................................................................

........................................................................................

........................................................................................

........................................................................................

# Day 179
## The Light of Men

*In him was life; and the life was the light of men.*
JOHN 1:4

God said, "Let there be light: and there was light" (Genesis 1:3). All life proceeds from our Lord, and all light, also. The Word is a life-and light-giving Word—"The light of the world is Jesus." Visualize the whole world in the darkness of sin, men groping blindly, restless and hopeless. *We* have the Light of Life. *We* see Him face-to-face. *We* bask in the sunshine of His glory. Pity the blind! Pray for the blind! Carry the light of the glorious Gospel to their darkened souls. Tell them to rise up and shine, for the Light has come and the glory of the Lord will shine on them.

*Help us, Lord, to walk in the light as we have fellowship with You and with one another. Amen.*

.................................................................................

.................................................................................

.................................................................................

.................................................................................

# Day 180

## The True Light

*That was the true Light, which lighteth*
*every man that cometh into the world.*
JOHN 1:9

"The *true* Light." This is in contrast with *false* lights. How many there are in our day. Satan is busy sending them out through false cults, false teachers, and false teaching. False lights dazzle the eyes but never reveal truth, nor bring radiance to the soul. The gloom of sin, the uncertainty of life, the dark outlook for the future confront the sinner stumbling along without God and without hope. God has ordained us as lights. Let our lights shine today, and may we help some blinded ones to see Jesus as the true Light of the World.

*Lord Jesus, in the light of Your Word, and in the light of Yourself,*
*may we witness for You today. Amen.*

# Day 184

## *The Only Begotten of the Father*

*And the Word was made flesh, and dwelt among us,*
*(and we beheld his glory, the glory as of the only begotten*
*of the Father,) full of grace and truth.*
JOHN 1:14

This is the most sublime of all the statements of scripture—"God became flesh!" John saw His glory. How wonderful! That glory was manifest in the person of the Only Begotten of the Father—Jesus Christ. He is the Unique Figure in the world's history—the sinless, perfect One—perfect God and perfect Man. "Great is the mystery of godliness: God was manifest in the flesh" (1 Timothy 3:16). He must be God to forgive sin, and He must be Man to atone for sin. So the God-Man is our Savior.

*We worship You, we adore You, O only begotten of the Father.*
*Help us to walk and talk with You today. Amen.*

# Day 182

## The Lamb of God

*The next day John seeth Jesus coming unto him, and saith,*
*Behold the Lamb of God, which taketh away the sin of the world.*
JOHN 4:29

How shall we say in a few words what springs up in our hearts and would break out from our lips? "The Lamb which taketh away our sin" is a better rendering, for He takes it away by *bearing* it. He *bore* the sins of those who received Him while here on the earth, and he bore them *away* when He paid the penalty on the cross and shed His atoning blood. *God's* Lamb! No one else could be God's Lamb. He was the *voluntary* offering. What can we do? Believe it, accept it, take our place with Him.

*Let us look on You every day—Jesus, Lamb of God—counting nothing*
*too good to give to You or too much to do for You. Amen.*

.............................................................................................................

.............................................................................................................

.............................................................................................................

.............................................................................................................

# Day 183
## The Son of God

*And I saw, and bare record that this is the Son of God.*
JOHN 1:34

John had not known Him as the Messiah although he did know Him to be Mary's son. But when the Holy Spirit descended on Jesus at His baptism, John knew Him as the Son of God and bore record to the fact. The testimony of John the Baptist is clear! Jesus is God's Son. He is the Promised One. Not *a* Son of God, as some of our learned critics condescendingly say, but *the* Son of God. We should seek to be like John the Baptist—a signpost pointing to Him and saying, "Behold! the Son of God." John laid down his life for his loyalty to the Son of God. May we be willing to suffer anything so that our testimony will be clear and clean always for Him.

*Lord, help us to point someone to You today. Amen.*

.......................................................................................................................

.......................................................................................................................

.......................................................................................................................

.......................................................................................................................

# Day 184

## *Rabbi*

*Nathanael answered and saith unto him, Rabbi,*
*thou art the Son of God; thou art the King of Israel.*
JOHN 1:49

*Rabbi* means "teacher" and is used seven times in the New Testament.
Nathanael recognized Christ as a teacher and He was—the greatest
Teacher that ever lived. A careful study of the four Gospels with a
mind-set of learning how Christ taught, His method, His manner,
and His purpose, is better than any other possible training for Bible
teachers. Christ was a true teacher. He taught the truth. He lowered
himself to men of low estate. He used words which men could
understand. He illustrated His messages in a practical manner. "The
common people heard him gladly" (Mark 12:37). That was a high
compliment indeed.

*Lord, help us to teach by our lips and by our life.*
*Let us pray that we may teach like that today. Amen.*

...............................................................................................................

...............................................................................................................

...............................................................................................................

...............................................................................................................

# Day 185
## The King of Israel

*Nathanael answered and saith unto him, Rabbi. . .*
*thou art the King of Israel.*
JOHN 4:49

When Philip found Nathanael, the latter said to him, "Can there any good thing come out of Nazareth?" (John 4:46) But when Nathanael came in touch with Jesus he broke out in testimony to His deity and His Messiahship. Our Lord did not fail to acknowledge this sterling testimony and a great promise was given to Nathanael, "Hereafter ye shall see heaven open, and the angels of God ascending and descending" (John 4:54). Ministering spirits were to be seen by him. Prayers were to ascend in the name of Christ and answers were to come back through Christ. We also can see the open heavens if we have faith.

*Let us send up our prayers today in His name*
*and look for the answer. Amen.*

.............................................................................................................................

.............................................................................................................................

.............................................................................................................................

.............................................................................................................................

# Day 186

## His Only Begotten Son

*For God so loved the world, that he gave his only begotten Son,*
*that whosoever believeth in him should not perish,*
*but have everlasting life.*

JOHN 3:16

Here is the most beloved verse in the Bible. What a revelation of God, of Christ, of the depths and power of love! How could He? Abraham gave his son, and God graciously gave him back. But *God's Son*—the Son of His love—the Only Begotten One—was given to a lost world, to sinful men. How did He give Him? Clothed in human form—a Man! Oh, the wonders of such a love! How it should stir our hearts! How we should love God for His gift! How we should love our Lord Jesus Christ—God's Only Begotten Son!

*Let us with throbbing hearts for a lost world go out today,*
*and all the days, to tell the story to sinful, suffering men. Amen.*

........................................................................................

........................................................................................

........................................................................................

........................................................................................

# Day 187
## The Gift of God

*Jesus answered and said unto her, If thou knewest the gift of God, and who it is that saith to thee, Give me to drink; thou wouldest have asked of him, and he would have given thee living water.*

JOHN 4:10

Here is that wonderful scene at the well of Samaria. The Lord has gone out of His way to meet the poor, sinful woman who has come to the well at a time when other women would not come; heavyhearted, hopeless, but *One* loved her with a holy love. He is there and reveals Himself as the "Gift of God." He is God's gift to us. What is our gift to Him? May we yield ourselves and all we are and have to Him!

*May we imitate the Samaritan woman and go out with the message: Come, see a Man—God's Gift. Amen.*

.......................................................................................

.......................................................................................

.......................................................................................

.......................................................................................

# Day 188

## *Messiah*

*The woman saith unto him, I know that Messias cometh,
which is called Christ: when he is come, he will tell us all things.*
JOHN 4:25

There is no book like the Bible, and there never can be. Christ's
interview with the woman at the well and His revelation of Himself
is unique and contrary to any conception that could have been made
of Him. The Samaritans, as did the Jews, anticipated a Christ (an
Anointed One). This was the promise given in Deuteronomy 18:18.
This woman was the last one we would have chosen for such a
revelation—but her soul was filled at once with the Spirit of life and
hope, and her lips bore a testimony—humiliating to herself—but
bringing salvation to a multitude. Oh, that our lips might bear such
convincing, convicting, and converting testimony.

*Lord, make us like this Samaritan woman! Amen.*

.......................................................................................................................

.......................................................................................................................

.......................................................................................................................

.......................................................................................................................

# Day 189

## The Christ, the Savior of the World

*We have heard him ourselves, and know that this*
*is indeed the Christ, the Saviour of the world.*
JOHN 4:42

The testimony of one woman brings from the lips of many this title, "Christ, the Savior of the world." For a two days' revival, Christ remained in the little city of the Samaritans, and there was a blessed first fruitage to His glory. These people, unlike the Jews, asked for no signs, no miracles. They took Him at His word, just as we must do. When He speaks, it is God that speaks. "We have heard him ourselves." The need of the world today is the personal experience of believers manifested in a personal devotion to Christ and in personal testimony to a hungry-hearted world.

*Oh Christ, Savior of the world, baptize us*
*with the Spirit of service for You! Amen.*

..........................................................................................................................

..........................................................................................................................

..........................................................................................................................

..........................................................................................................................

# Day 190
## The True Bread from Heaven

*My Father giveth you the true bread from heaven.*
JOHN 6:32

There had been a wonderful scene on the lakeside. A great multitude of people had wound their way around the lake to meet Jesus, and after a day of preaching, they were hungry and had no food. A little boy was used of God to bring about a great miracle. Five thousand men—beside the women and children—were fed and twelve baskets of fragments gathered. Moses, by God's power, brought daily bread from heaven, but it was only temporal. Jesus is the *True* Bread from heaven which, if men partake of, they live forever. Only He can satisfy our soul's hunger. The world is starving for the True Bread.

*Lord Jesus, help us to go out today and feed some hungry souls. Amen.*

# Day 191
## *The Bread of God*

*For the bread of God is he which cometh down from heaven,
and giveth life unto the world.*
JOHN 6:33

In this verse Jesus reveals Himself as coming down from heaven. The
Bread of God is a gift to hungry humanity—a divine gift—a heavenly
gift—a gift from God—a gift spiritual and supernatural. Teachers,
preachers, and workers for the Lord must always bear this in mind:
The unsaved are hungry. Nothing will ever satisfy their hunger but
the Bread of God—Jesus Christ. "He satisfieth the longing soul, and
filleth the hungry soul with goodness (God-likeness)" (Psalm 107:9).

*Help us, Lord, to hear the cry of the hungry souls all around us,
and help us to minister to them, in Your name. Amen.*

.......................................................................................................................................

.......................................................................................................................................

.......................................................................................................................................

.......................................................................................................................................

# Day 192
## *The Bread of Life*

*And Jesus said unto them, I am the bread of life: he that cometh to me shall never hunger; and he that believeth on me shall never thirst.*
JOHN 6:35

Answering humanity's cry as embodied in the request "Lord, evermore give us this bread," Jesus says: "I am the Bread of Life," i.e., the Life-eternal-giving Bread. This reply settles the question forever. He is the *True Bread*, the *Bread of God*, and the *Bread of Life*. How is this Bread to be dispensed? It must be made known to an ignorant world. The terms which it is to be received must be made clear and definite. "Come to me," says Jesus, "and you shall never hunger. Believe in me and you shall never thirst." How simple! The "life gift" is a *love* gift. Never put a straw in the way of a hungry sinner. There is nothing to do but to believe—receive—accept. Nothing more.

*Lord, help us to go out laden with the Bread of Life and give it to the hungry. Amen.*

..................................................................................................

..................................................................................................

..................................................................................................

..................................................................................................

# Day 193
## The Living Bread

*I am the living bread which came down from heaven.*
JOHN 6:51

Here is the fourth assertion of our Lord concerning Himself as the "Bread of Heaven," the "True Bread," the "Bread of God," the "Bread of Life," and now the "Living Bread." And He tells us that He will lay down His own life in order that we may have this Living Bread to eat and so live forever. The process by which we are to nourish the new nature which we received by accepting Him is by feeding on Him. If our bodies do not take in food, they perish, and in the proportion that we do take in our food, we are able-bodied. Here is a searching lesson: Many believers are not strong. Paul says, "For this cause many are weak and sickly among you, and many sleep" (1 Corinthians 11:30).

*Lord, make us strong through feeding on Yourself. Amen.*

# Day 194

## *The Light of the World*

*Then spake Jesus again unto them, saying,
I am the light of the world: he that followeth me shall not
walk in darkness, but shall have the light of life.*

JOHN 8:12

"And God said, Let there be light: and there was light" (Genesis 1:3).
And "God divided the light from the darkness" (Genesis 1:4). Now
our Lord says, "I am the Light of the World." The world is a dark,
gloomy place, but "God is light, and in him is no darkness at all"
(1 John 1:5). If we follow Him we will not walk in darkness. "Walking
in the light," we have fellowship with one another and reflect the glory
of His person in the gloom of the world. "Arise, shine; for thy light is
come, and the glory of the LORD is risen upon thee" (Isaiah 60:1). He
can only be manifested through the lives of His own and the light of
the Word.

*O, Lord of Light, shine in our hearts and through our lives. Amen.*

.......................................................................................................

.......................................................................................................

.......................................................................................................

.......................................................................................................

# Day 195
## I Am

*Jesus said unto them, Verily, verily, I say unto you,*
*Before Abraham was, I am.*
JOHN 8:58

The life of Abraham was limited. We know the time of his birth and of his death. But there is no time limit to the life of our Lord. "Before Abraham was, I am." He was the Eternal Son of God. He was the Uncreated One, the Eternal One, the Self-existent One. Before the creation of the world He was the "I Am!" After the world passes away He will still be the "I Am." Without Him nothing was made that was made. He was God! Wonder of wonders! God manifest in the flesh! God pleading with men! God on the cross! God in the glory and coming in the clouds! Great, great is the mystery of God!

*Son of God, Son of man, at the right hand of the Glory,*
*we bow in Your presence and say with deepest reverence,*
*"Hallowed be Thy name." Amen.*

# Day 196

## The Door of the Sheep

*Then said Jesus unto them again, Verily, verily,
I say unto you, I am the door of the sheep.*
JOHN 10:7

What contrast could be greater than that between the "I Am" and this
title, "Door of the sheep"? Here our Lord paints a picture and uses
an allegory into which sheep, fold, and shepherd are introduced, He
Himself claiming a peculiar position, "The Door of the sheep." He
is the door by which entrance is gained to heaven. "By me if any man
enter in, he shall be saved." Put your hand on the door—Jesus Christ
on the cross—and enter the fold. There is safety. There is liberty.
There is food for the sheep, and water and rest. Free from Satan's
snare, filled with joy and peace, what more could we ask or desire?

*Dear Lord, shepherd us today in Your own arms. Amen.*

# Day 197
## *The Good Shepherd*

*I am the good shepherd:*
*the good shepherd giveth his life for the sheep.*
JOHN 10:11

We shall have several meditations on our Lord as Shepherd, but here He speaks of Himself as the *"Good* Shepherd." God is good and Jesus is God. Therefore, He is good. If we could stop for a few moments and sense His presence, longing to speak to us in tones of deepest love, with His wonderful eyes fixed on us, and His holy desire to draw us in loving tenderness to Himself—would we not say of Him, "He is so good. He died for me"? And would our hearts not go out in passionate love to Him?

*Loving Shepherd, help us to keep close to You today. Amen.*

.......................................................................................................................

.......................................................................................................................

.......................................................................................................................

.......................................................................................................................

# Day 198
## *One Shepherd*

*And other sheep I have, which are not of this fold:*
*them also I must bring, and they shall hear my voice;*
*and there shall be one fold, and one shepherd.*
JOHN 10:16

Israel had a limited view of our Christ. They were wrapped up in themselves. Selfish, narrow in their vision of the Messiah that was to come, they were without compassion, as we ourselves so often are, having no patience with those who differ from us. Not so with our Lord. He had a heart boundless in love; a soul longing for the children of men; looking forward into the future, seeing the hatred of the Jews (His own people) to the cross, the cruel death, and then the many sheep, washed in the same blood, filled with the same Holy Spirit of Life, folded in the *one fold*. Wonderful vision!

*Shepherd of our lives, enlarge our hearts in sympathy with*
*the pulsing of Your own loving heart. Amen.*

......................................................................................................................

......................................................................................................................

......................................................................................................................

......................................................................................................................

# Day 199

## The Resurrection

*Jesus said unto her, I am the resurrection, and the life:*
*be that believeth in me, though he were dead, yet shall he live.*
JOHN 11:25

Here our Lord links His own title "I Am" with the resurrection, "I am
the gift of the resurrection to all who believe on me. Though he die,
who believeth on me, yet shall he live." Faith in Him equals eternal
life and that assures our resurrection. Because He lives, we *must* live.
Death may come to us, but it will be the shadow only, which will pass
and leave us in the full sunlight of eternal life. Nothing can separate
us. He who raised up Christ from the dead will revive our bodies.
"Whosoever liveth and believeth in me shall never die" (John 11:26).
In His resurrection He conquered death. Praise the Lord!

*Lord Jesus, come quickly and change these bodies of our abasement*
*into the likeness of Your own glorified body. Amen.*

# Day 200

## *The Christ, the Son of God*

*She saith unto him, Yea, Lord:*
*I believe that thou art the Christ, the Son of God.*
JOHN 11:27

Here is a remarkable confession from the lips of Martha, "The Christ, the Son of God." Lazarus was in the tomb. Her eyes, no doubt, were full of tears, her soul full of sorrow, but her faith in Jesus as the Christ never wavered. She heard that Jesus was coming and called Him "Lord"; then she said, "I believe that thou art the Christ, the Son of God." How sweet! How blessed! But yet the heart of Jesus was pained, for He groaned in spirit because of her lack of faith that He would answer prayer and raise up Lazarus.

*Lord Jesus, help us never to disappoint You in our faith in*
*Your power and Your promise to answer our faith. Amen.*

.................................................................................................................................

.................................................................................................................................

.................................................................................................................................

.................................................................................................................................

# Day 204

## A Grain of Wheat

*And Jesus answered them, saying, The hour is come, that the Son of man should be glorified. Verily, verily, I say unto you, Except a corn {grain} of wheat fall into the ground and die, it abideth alone: but if it die, it bringeth forth much fruit.*

JOHN 12:23–24

Before He could be glorified He must be as a grain of wheat. How insignificant seems a grain of wheat, and yet this suggestion is one of the most wonderful in the Word of God. A grain of wheat is so small that it can hardly be held between the fingers without dropping, and yet it is associated with *His glory*. He must die in order to bring forth fruit. So must we, if we are to be like Him. How hard it seems to human pride to become as a grain of wheat and then to die to this world. But listen to the words of His testimony and look on His example. Do we desire to be like Him?

*Lord, help us to ponder on this truth today
and long to be more like You. Amen.*

...................................................................................................................

...................................................................................................................

...................................................................................................................

...................................................................................................................

# Day 202
## *Master*

*Ye call me Master and Lord: and ye say well; for so I am.*
JOHN 13:13

"Master" means "Teacher" and the authoritative Teacher He was and is. We are to learn from Him, for He is the Truth and reveals the truth to men. He has left to us His words of wisdom, and we are to sit at His feet and learn from Him. We recognize this position as our Lord by yielding submission to His authority and acknowledging it daily. He knows the past. He knows the present. He knows the future. Let our prayer be

*Lord, teach us Your will, through Your Word. Help us to know, understand, and gladly live out Your will. Amen.*

.......................................................................................................................

.......................................................................................................................

.......................................................................................................................

.......................................................................................................................

# Day 203
## *The Way*

*Jesus saith unto him, I am the way.*
JOHN 14:6

He is the Way—"a Way without deviation"—the straight and narrow Way, the only Way which leads directly to the Father. There are a thousand ways which lead to destruction, to eternal darkness and separation from the Father. Satan has multiplied agents pointing to his wicked way, but Christ is the Signpost, saying: "This is the Way; walk ye in it." When we walk in *the Way* we walk in the light. We journey with Him in sweet fellowship. What a joyful journey! The Way is lightened by His countenance. He holds us by the hand. He supplies our needs. What a Savior!

*Lord, help us to keep in touch with You as we travel along the heavenly highway to the home prepared for us by You. Amen.*

.................................................................................................................

.................................................................................................................

.................................................................................................................

.................................................................................................................

# Day 204
## *The Truth*

*Jesus saith unto him, I am. . .the truth.*
JOHN 14:6

He is not only the Way, but He is the *Truth*—"the truth without any contradiction." We are God's free men, for we know Him who is the Truth, and the Truth makes us free. He is the Truth about the Word of God. Hear Him say, "I am not come to destroy the law or the prophets, but to fulfill." And "It is easier for heaven and earth to pass than for one jot or tittle of the law to fail." Pity the poor deceived students in the schools and the devil-deluded ministers and teachers who cast any reflection on the Word of God to which Jesus has set His eternal seal! Doubt concerning the inerrancy of the Bible is a doubt concerning Himself. Do not taint your soul with such unholy thoughts.

*Lord, You are the Truth. We look to You.*
*Guide us into the Truth every day. Amen.*

......................................................................................................

......................................................................................................

......................................................................................................

......................................................................................................

# Day 205
## The Life

*Jesus saith unto him, I am. . .the life.*
JOHN 14:6

He is not only the Way and the Truth, but He is the Life—Eternal
Life, the Author of Life, and the Giver of Life. We almost stagger
when we confront this statement by the One who left heaven and the
throne of God and came to this earth that He might reveal Himself
and receive to Himself those who were to inherit through Him and
share with Him this eternal Life. Our short pilgrimage here is soon
ended and then, O joy, we enter the unending, eternal Life.

*Lord, how we thank You that You are our eternal Life*
*through the indwelling Holy Spirit. Amen.*

.................................................................................................................

.................................................................................................................

.................................................................................................................

.................................................................................................................

# Day 206
## The Vine

*I am the vine, ye are the branches: He that abideth in me,*
*and I in him, the same bringeth forth much fruit:*
*for without me ye can do nothing.*
JOHN 15:5

Here the Lord calls Himself "The Vine" as He associates Himself
with the branches. He is the root and stem on which we, as branches,
must depend. The purpose of the Vine is to bear fruit. The life is in
the *vine*, but that life is also in the branches, and we are to be fruit-
bearing branches. "He that *abideth* in me, and I in him, the same
bringeth forth much fruit." We can bear no fruit of ourselves. Our
dependence is on Him. The desire of the Husbandman is to produce
fruit, and we must ask ourselves the question: "Am I a fruit-bearing
branch? If not, why not?" How patient He is, yet how fearful is the
contemplation of the thought: "I may be a fruitless branch."

*Lord, forbid that it should be so. Holy Spirit, fill us with Yourself*
*that we may bear much fruit. Amen.*

# Day 207
## *The Overcomer*

*I have overcome the world.*
JOHN 16:33

A graphic picture—one of the "last night messages" of our Lord—fraught with tremendous interest to every believer. A world of tribulation confronted Him, and a world of tribulation confronts His church. "Ye shall have tribulation" and we do, but in Him we have peace—the peace of God, which surpasses understanding. How blessed to be in Him who is the Source of our strength! We must learn to overcome through Him. There is nothing too hard for Him. He loves to give us victory. We please Him by trusting Him and taking by faith what He has purchased for us.

*Let us bow in His presence and commit all to Him for victory today and thus glorify our Overcomer. Amen.*

.................................................................................

.................................................................................

.................................................................................

.................................................................................

# Day 208
## Our Keeper

*While I was with them in the world, I kept them in thy name:*
*those that thou gavest me I have kept.*

JOHN 17:12

This prayer on the night before His crucifixion is one of sacred sweetness and comfort. While He was here He guarded and kept His own. Now He is in the glory and still guards and keeps us. The enemy, Satan, who captured and controlled Judas, would separate us, if he could, from our Lord; but He is our Keeper and we can trust in His unfailing promise: "I will him keep in perfect peace whose mind is stayed on me because he trusteth in me." The devil has ten thousand agents seeking to spoil our lives, but nothing can separate us from the love of God as manifested in Christ Jesus our Lord.

*"Now unto him who is able to keep us from falling. . .*
*to the only wise God, our Savior, be glory, forever."* Amen.

# Day 209
## *The Sent of the Father*

*As thou hast sent me into the world,*
*even so have I also sent them into the world.*
JOHN 17:18

From the glory which He had with the Father before the world was,
He was sent into this world of sin and shame to redeem sinful men.
He was God's Apostle—God's "Sent One." His prayer now to the
Father is that they might be *sanctified* (set apart) as He was set apart
for the work of redemption. He prays that His disciples might also
be set apart for the great work of saving men. Christ has not changed.
This prayer was for us, also, as He says in verse 20: "Neither pray I
for these alone, but for them also which shall believe on me through
their word." His holy desire is that we might be in the world with the
same message that He Himself had.

*Lord Jesus, help us to recognize today Your*
*call and our calling to save souls. Amen.*

..................................................................................................................

..................................................................................................................

..................................................................................................................

..................................................................................................................

# Day 210
## The Man

*Behold the man!*
JOHN 19:5

"Behold the Man!" How little Pilate knew what he was doing when he bestowed on our Lord that significant title, "The Man!" The word "man" is used nearly three thousand times in the Bible, but there is only one "The Man"—the Man from heaven. The word in the original is "Adam"—a human being—and such He was. Oh, the marvel of it! It seems too good to be true, and yet it is true. For our sakes—in order to be one with us and to bear our sin—He threw aside His royal vesture and donned the garments of humanity, that He might interpret to us the purpose of the Father.

*In the name of this Man, our Father, we ask for guidance today and pray that our hearts may be in tune with His. Amen.*

.......................................................................................................................

.......................................................................................................................

.......................................................................................................................

.......................................................................................................................

# Day 244
## My Lord and My God

*And Thomas answered and said unto him, My Lord and my God.*
JOHN 20:28

Thomas is the doubting disciple. He loved His Lord and had
been willing to die with Him but could not believe in His bodily
resurrection. He demanded a definite proof. Eight days had passed
when he is confronted with the risen Jesus who says, "Reach hither
thy finger, and behold my hands; and reach hither thy hand, and
thrust it into my side: and be not faithless, but believing," and out of
a heart throbbing with joy Thomas cries, "My Lord and my God."
How sympathetically loving is our Lord with our unbelief. How
patient He is, yet how He longs for our unquestioning, implicit faith.
Let us honor Him by believing in Him with all our heart.

*Our Lord and our God, help us today to look on the
wounds which You bore for us and with full faith
renew our pledge of loyalty to You. Amen.*

.................................................................................................................

.................................................................................................................

.................................................................................................................

.................................................................................................................

# Day 242
## A Man Approved of God

*Jesus of Nazareth, a man approved of God among you by miracles and wonders and signs, which God did by him in the midst of you.*
ACTS 2:22

This is the testimony of Peter, the fisherman-apostle, concerning our Lord, Jesus of Nazareth. "A man approved of God!" He professed to be the promised Messiah, the Son of God, and proved His profession by His public life. His miraculous works were the proof of miraculous power. He was God in human form. He set His followers the example for holy living. When believers are anointed of the Holy Spirit and seek by lip and life to honor their Lord, the approval of God the Father will be on them.

*Lord, help us to live a life approved of God, so that through us, wonders may be wrought in the salvation of souls. Amen.*

........................................................................................................................

........................................................................................................................

........................................................................................................................

........................................................................................................................

# Day 213
## *Thine Holy One*

*Because thou wilt not leave my soul in hell,*
*neither wilt thou suffer thine Holy One to see corruption.*
ACTS 2:27

The Godhead and manhood were united in Christ, and it was impossible that He should be held by the power of death. He passed through the agony; He paid the penalty; He suffered the separation; but death could not hold Him. The unfailing Word of God had promised His resurrection and so "up from the grave he arose." He hath broken the bars of death for us and in the freedom of the new life, with glorified bodies, we will be forever with Him.

*May our souls be led to magnify You, the Holy One,*
*today and rejoice in the hope of soon being with You. Amen.*

..................................................................................................................

..................................................................................................................

..................................................................................................................

..................................................................................................................

# Day 214

## The Holy One and Just

*But ye denied the Holy One and the Just,
and desired a murderer to be granted unto you.*
ACTS 3:14

Peter is delivering a sermon to the Jews. They had looked with wonder at the lame man healed by the hand of Peter, and Peter was taking advantage of the opportunity to set before them the resurrected Christ as the One whom they had condemned but whom God had raised from the dead, to whom he gives this title "Holy One and Just." And such is He, the Spotless One, without sin, God manifest in the flesh. Do *we* recognize him as the Holy One? Sometimes familiarity breeds indifference. May it never be so with us. Every suggestion of the "Holy One" should stir our souls in adoration and holy desire to be like Him.

*Oh Holy One, may we seek earnestly today to live
in Your sight, adoring You constantly. Amen.*

......................................................................................................

......................................................................................................

......................................................................................................

......................................................................................................

# Day 215

## The Prince of Life

*And killed the Prince of life, whom God hath raised*
*from the dead; whereof we are witnesses.*
ACTS 3:15

"The Prince of Life"—a remarkable title to give to our Lord when viewed in contrast with Barabbas, the murderer who took life. One— the bestower of life; the other—the destroyer of life. He came that men might have life and life more abundantly. How many there are who ignore and reject Him, who will never have the joy of living and reigning with Him through the eternal ages. Are we doing our best to make Him known to lost men?

*Lord Jesus, Prince of Life, stir our hearts with compassion for the lost, and help us today to make You known to a blinded soul. Amen.*

..............................................................................................................................

..............................................................................................................................

..............................................................................................................................

..............................................................................................................................

# Day 246

## The Holy Child Jesus

*For of a truth against thy holy child Jesus, whom thou hast anointed,
both Herod, and Pontius Pilate, with the Gentiles,
and the people of Israel, were gathered together.*

ACTS 4:27

Peter and John are before the Council to be examined in connection
with the miracle of the healing of the lame man. They gave their
testimony to the fact that it was in the despised name of Jesus Christ
of Nazareth that this had been done. The Council could do nothing
but let them go. They went at once to the place where the church were
gathered together and reported what had been done and the assembly
lifted their voices in thanksgiving, glorifying the name of the Holy
Child Jesus against whom His enemies were gathered. They prayed
that in the name of this Holy Child Jesus signs and wonders might be
worked and they were.

*Lord Jesus, we thank You that miracles are being worked today
and will be until You come again. Amen.*

.................................................................................................

.................................................................................................

.................................................................................................

.................................................................................................

# Day 217

## A Prince and a Savior

*Him hath God exalted with his right hand*
*to be a Prince and a Saviour.*
ACTS 5:31

Here is a picture and a theme for our meditation. A convict—a criminal in the sight of men—hanging on a tree, dying an awful death of shame, suffering the agonies of hell itself that the question of sinful man's sin might be settled forever—exalted by God to the highest heights—a Prince! But to establish His title He became the Sin-bearer that He might become the Sin-blotter. Destined to deepest depths of human suffering and humility, but raised to the highest heights of honor and glory. Oh, the wretchedness of our sin which demanded it, and the wonders of a Savior which delivered it!

*Lord Jesus, our Prince and our Savior,*
*we yield ourselves to You with glad hearts. Amen.*

..................................................................................................................

..................................................................................................................

..................................................................................................................

..................................................................................................................

# Day 248

## The Just One

*Which of the prophets have not your fathers persecuted? and they have slain them which shewed before of the coming of the Just One; of whom ye have been now the betrayers and murderers.*

ACTS 7:52

The words "Just (righteous) One" burst from the lips of Stephen, the first martyr, in the wonderful message which he gave before the Council in defending the name and glory of our Lord Jesus Christ. He paid with his life for his loyalty to his Lord and will receive his reward. It was through his testimony that the Spirit of God brought conviction to Saul of Tarsus, resulting in his conversion. How much would *we* be willing to suffer for Him?

*Oh, blessed Savior of our souls, warm our hearts in devotion to You. Make us sturdy and strong as defenders of the faith. Amen.*

.............................................................................................................

.............................................................................................................

.............................................................................................................

.............................................................................................................

# Day 249

## *Lord Jesus*

*And they stoned Stephen, calling upon God,
and saying, Lord Jesus, receive my spirit.*
ACTS 7:59

Stephen is passing through the fire of Jewish hatred. But God is faithful to His faithful servant and martyr and opens the heavens to him showing him Jesus standing at the right hand of His glory. The cry of Stephen was "Lord Jesus, receive my spirit." His prayer was like that of Jesus who said, "Father, into thy hands I commend my spirit" (Luke 23:46). What a testimony to the deity of our Lord! Only He who gave the spirit could receive it. To depart and be with Christ was far better for Stephen, and it will be for us when in His own good time He calls us.

*Lord Jesus, help us to witness a good confession,
gladly facing any foe, even death, that like Stephen,
we may glorify You whether in life or death. Amen.*

........................................................................................................

........................................................................................................

........................................................................................................

........................................................................................................

# Day 220
## Lord of All

*The word which God sent unto the children of Israel,*
*preaching peace by Jesus Christ: (he is Lord of all).*
ACTS 10:36

Jesus Christ is Lord of all men. Peter was a Jew and did not want to depart from Jewish ground, but God sent him a vision from heaven to make clear to him that He was no respecter of persons. "While Peter yet spake these words, the Holy Ghost fell on all them which heard the word." Our Lord loves all; He died for all; He commissions us to go and preach to all. The world is the field, and every soul living has a claim on us, which we must meet and answer for. What a wonderful Lord of all! What a wonderful Gospel! What a wonderful salvation!

*Oh Lord of all, rebuke us today for our selfishness,*
*our lack of likeness to You, and fill us with the Holy Ghost*
*that we may gladly be witnesses to all men. Amen.*

.............................................................................................................

.............................................................................................................

.............................................................................................................

.............................................................................................................

# Day 224

## The Judge of Quick and Dead

*And he commanded us to preach unto the people, and to testify that it is he which was ordained of God to be the Judge of quick and dead.*
ACTS 10:42

Here is a testimony to the fact of the resurrection of the dead and a judgment of the living and the dead of all generations. Christ's position is one of dignity and power and must be recognized. In love for men, He became a Man, mingled with men, manifested His love for individuals as well as for all men—but it must not be forgotten that He is also the *Judge* of all men. Believers have rights and titles conferred on them by reason of their acceptance of the sacrifice of Jesus Christ, but they, too, must face Him to be judged for their works. *The Day* must come and we must face it.

*Lord, we are Yours and You are ours.*
*Let us adore and serve You today. Amen.*

# Day 222
## *That Man Whom He Hath Ordained*

*Because he hath appointed a day, in the which he will judge the world in righteousness by that man whom he hath ordained.*
ACTS 17:31

Jesus was ordained—set apart—appointed—designated—as the Man who is to judge the whole human race, and the evidence, or proof, of this is the fact of His resurrection from the dead. It will be a righteous judgment by a righteous Judge. It will be an impartial judgment by One who created all things and who knows all things, a holy, unerring Judge. He will have the books opened before Him, and there can never be any appeal from the verdict. What is your relation to this Ordained Man? Are you ready?

*Lord, help us to be faithful witnesses while it is called today. Amen.*

.........................................................................................................................

.........................................................................................................................

.........................................................................................................................

.........................................................................................................................

# Day 223
## *Jesus of Nazareth*

*And I answered, Who art thou, Lord? And he said unto me,
I am Jesus of Nazareth, whom thou persecutest.*
ACTS 22:8

More than twenty times in the scriptures our Lord is called "Jesus
of Nazareth." Here it is remarkable. Paul is telling the story of his
conversion. He is bound with chains, a prisoner in the hands of the
Roman authorities. He says that the words which came to him from
the heavens were "Saul, Saul, why persecutest thou me?" And in
answer to his question "Who art thou, Lord?" came the answer,
"I am Jesus of Nazareth." That is His name *now*. From the glory He
acknowledges His earthly title—"Jesus of Nazareth." Jesus is God.
He made the worlds, but He acknowledges the little obscure town of
Nazareth, His hometown on earth.

*Jesus of Nazareth, we want to be one with You.
Guide us to Your glory. Amen.*

........................................................................................................

........................................................................................................

........................................................................................................

........................................................................................................

# Day 224

## Jesus Christ Our Lord

*That as sin hath reigned unto death, even so might grace reign through righteousness unto eternal life by Jesus Christ our Lord.*
ROMANS 5:24

Here we have the grouping of three titles, "Jesus" (Savior) "Christ" (Anointed) "Lord" (Master). In a few words the great problem of the ages is solved. Sin, with its death-dealing power, wore the crown of victory over mortal man, but there was One greater than Satan, the author of sin, and in that One was manifested the victorious power of grace (unmerited favor) by which, through the sacrifice of Jesus Christ, God's condescending love could be manifested in His Son, our Lord and Master.

*"Jesus Christ, our Lord"–we breathe the words with joyful lips and give You thanks for that grace which has saved and which keeps us. Amen.*

......................................................................................................

......................................................................................................

......................................................................................................

......................................................................................................

# Day 225

## The Firstborn among Many Brethren

*For whom he did foreknow, he also did predestinate*
*to be conformed to the image of his Son, that he might be*
*the firstborn among many brethren.*
ROMANS 8:29

A wonderful title for our Lord, "The Firstborn!" Adam was the firstborn among men, but he forfeited his rights and privileges through sin and God ordained another Man to be the First, who was to be born of a woman and be the Head of a great company of brethren. God has plans for the human race and is carrying them out as the years come and go. Jesus is the "Firstborn," and we who are "born-again" ones are, by His grace, being conformed to His image, and when He comes from heaven we will be among the sons of God and united forever to and with Him.

*Our eyes are fastened on You, Firstborn One, today,*
*and we say from our hearts, come quickly. Amen.*

.............................................................................................................................

.............................................................................................................................

.............................................................................................................................

.............................................................................................................................

# Day 226

## His Own Son

*He that spared not his own Son, but delivered him up for us all,*
*how shall he not with him also freely give us all things?*
ROMANS 8:32

"His Own Son," "His Only Son," "The Son of His Love"—the dearest, the best He gave out of His great heart freely, lovingly, once for all to the sinful children of men. Having given us His best, will He withhold anything from us? Why do we doubt Him? Why do we live such poor, selfish, sordid lives, when the world is so needy, when hearts are so heavy and broken? Why do we fail to take hold of what He has so freely offered us? Is there not a challenge to us here? Let us meet it today.

*Lord, help us to believe and with joyful hearts ask for great things*
*for a needy world in the name of Your Son. Amen.*

# Day 227
## God Blessed Forever

*Whose are the fathers, and of whom as concerning the flesh Christ came, who is over all, God blessed for ever. Amen.*
ROMANS 9:5

As we journey through the Word of God, how Christ illumines it all with His presence! His titles are many. How significant is this "God blessed forever!" The promised Messiah of the Jewish stock and the flower of its race, yet they would not receive Him. He was the Shekinah glory dwelling in human form in the midst of the world. But their eyes were blinded, and what centuries of sorrow have followed and will follow until He comes for His own, and then will come the saddest of all experiences for them. Pity both Jew and Gentile in our own day who refuse to acknowledge Him as "God Blessed Forever."

*May we bow to Him today and say from our hearts, "To us You are indeed 'God Blessed Forever.'" Amen.*

.................................................................................................

.................................................................................................

.................................................................................................

.................................................................................................

# Day 228
## *Lord over All*

*For there is no difference between the Jew and the Greek:*
*for the same Lord over all is rich unto all that call upon him.*
ROMANS 10:12

"He is rich unto all that call upon him." Then why not call? The only
requirement is that we belong to His family. The door is open to all
to join that family, and for the family there are riches of revelation,
riches of forgiveness, riches of grace, riches of love. Just call in His
name, and He will answer, for "Whatsoever ye shall ask in my name,
that will I do"(John 14:13), and that word "whatsoever" comprehends
everything. He will supply *all* your need. How much we lose—because
we do not call.

*Lord over All, hear our prayer today. May we glory in the riches*
*of Your name, and will You lead us to believe and receive. Amen.*

.................................................................................................................

.................................................................................................................

.................................................................................................................

.................................................................................................................

# Day 229
## The Lord

*For whosoever shall call upon the name of the Lord shall be saved.*
ROMANS 10:13

The Master loves to hear the call of a sinner for salvation. How many sin-sick, weary souls there are who are hungry for salvation. They do not know this verse. They have false ideas about Christ and about salvation. They would gladly cry to the Lord, but He has not been revealed to them. They need someone to tell them of His longing to have them in His family. "Faith cometh by hearing, and hearing by the word of God" (Romans 10:17). Listen to the words "How beautiful are the feet of them that preach the gospel of peace, and bring glad tidings of good things" (Romans 10:15). "To preach" means "to tell out," "to proclaim"—and if you are a believer then you are a God-ordained preacher and will be held accountable for your ministry.

*Oh Lord, our Master, send us all out today*
*to tell the love story to others. Amen.*

........................................................................................................

........................................................................................................

........................................................................................................

........................................................................................................

# Day 230
## The Deliverer

*And so all Israel shall be saved: as it is written, There shall come out of Sion the Deliverer, and shall turn away ungodliness from Jacob.*
ROMANS 11:26

Here we face a startling prophecy. The ancient people of God, scattered about in every land without a country of their own except as certain permission is given them—as now to reside in the old land—these Jews are yet to be delivered and as a nation they will turn to Christ as their Deliverer and will be God's earthly people as we will be His heavenly people. Let us never forget how much we owe to the Jewish race, and let us seek earnestly to bring as many as possible of them to Christ now.

*Oh Lord Jesus, You have been our Deliverer. We glory in Your name. Help us to help others to know You. Amen.*

.......................................................................................

.......................................................................................

.......................................................................................

.......................................................................................

# Day 234

## Lord Both of the Dead and the Living

*For to this end Christ both died, and rose, and revived,*
*that he might be Lord both of the dead and living.*
ROMANS 14:9

Christ is the center of all affairs related to this earth. He rules. He reigns. He keeps books, and someday those books are to be opened. Adam and Eve and everyone that has ever lived will be there to answer to the call. Saints (or saved ones) will be judged for their manner of living. That will be one judgment. Sinners will be judged, and that will be another judgment. There can be no evasions, no exceptions. All accounts must be faced and settled. Men should live in that prospect. How blessed for those whose sins are covered by the blood! But how sorrowful for even those if they have not sought to do their best for Him!

*Oh Lord, may the words of our mouths and the thoughts of our*
*hearts be pleasing to You today. Amen.*

........................................................................................................

........................................................................................................

........................................................................................................

........................................................................................................

# Day 232
## Minister of the Circumcision

*Now I say that Jesus Christ was a minister of the circumcision for the truth of God, to confirm the promises made unto the fathers.*
ROMANS 15:8

Here again we have a title which unites in the Spirit both Jew and Gentile as partakers of the grace of God. He came to the Jews with His message of love, but they would not have Him. He turned to the Gentiles and some received Him. The Gospel of Jesus Christ is for all men, because all have sinned. He came for all. He loved all. He died for all. He longs to gather all to Himself. He is the "Minister of the Circumcision" and the "Minister of the Cross." We are one in Him.

*Oh blessed One, minister to us today and help us to minister to You. Amen.*

.......................................................................................................

.......................................................................................................

.......................................................................................................

.......................................................................................................

# Day 233
## *The Power of God*

*But unto them which are called, both Jews and Greeks,
Christ the power of God.*
1 CORINTHIANS 1:24

When we use the word "power," we are possessed with a strange
sensation. Every fiber of our beings is tense, and we think of might
and authority. So when we think of our Lord Jesus Christ we can
visualize Him as the Mighty One. From a powerhouse the electric
current issues and darkness is displaced by light; the engine is imbued
with life and moves the train carrying, maybe, the armies of a nation.
So our Lord Jesus Christ is the "Power of God," for all power is
committed to Him. He speaks and it is done! And this Powerful One
has said, "Ask, and ye shall receive" (John 16:24). How wonderful
that He should love us!

*Lord Jesus, we commend ourselves to You today and
rest in faith in the power of Your love for us. Amen.*

......................................................................................................

......................................................................................................

......................................................................................................

......................................................................................................

# Day 234
## The Wisdom of God

*But unto them which are called, both Jews and Greeks, Christ. . .the wisdom of God.*
1 CORINTHIANS 1:24

To those who are called, He is the Wisdom of God. The Bible teaches us that wisdom is the principal thing and, therefore, we should seek wisdom and Him who is the storehouse of wisdom. "Never man spake like this man" (John 7:46). "If any of you lack wisdom. . .let him ask in faith, nothing wavering" (James 1:5–6). "Giving doth not impoverish him." "The wisdom of this world is foolishness with God" (1 Corinthians 3:19). Then let us be wise and seek the wisdom that surpasses all understanding.

*Lord, as we face the duties and privileges of today, guide us by Your wisdom to Your praise and glory. Amen.*

.......................................................................................................................

.......................................................................................................................

.......................................................................................................................

.......................................................................................................................

# Day 235

## Righteousness

*But of him are ye in Christ Jesus,*
*who of God is made unto us. . .righteousness.*
1 CORINTHIANS 1:30

Righteousness is "rightness." We were all wrong and always wrong,
but in Him we are made right. All of our righteousness was like filthy
rags. There was nothing in us that would commend us to God and
never could be. But what a change when we are in Him and He is in
us. We are made sinless, *in Him*, for He bore all our sins and paid all
the penalty, and His righteousness is imputed to us. What a joy to be
*consciously* in Him! And what a price He paid in order to become our
righteousness!

*Lord, teach us to recognize our unworthiness today and to dwell*
*much on the fact that You are our Righteousness. Amen.*

..............................................................................................................................................

..............................................................................................................................................

..............................................................................................................................................

..............................................................................................................................................

# Day 236

## *Sanctification*

*But of him are ye in Christ Jesus,*
*who of God is made unto us. . .sanctification.*
1 CORINTHIANS 1:30

To be "sanctified" is to be "separated"—"set apart." We could never be sanctified by our own efforts, for we are absolutely helpless except that He becomes all things to us. We are in Christ Jesus and what He is, we are, and what He has, we share. We are nothing. You are everything. Help us to see ourselves in Christ Jesus. You have set us apart to be Your representatives in a lost world. In every act and deed we represent You.

*Lord, today, may the words of our mouths and the meditations*
*of our hearts be acceptable unto You. Amen.*

....................................................................................................

....................................................................................................

....................................................................................................

....................................................................................................

# Day 237

## *Redemption*

*But of him are ye in Christ Jesus,*
*who of God is made unto us. . .redemption.*
1 CORINTHIANS 1:30

What an awful thing is sin, and to "come short of the glory of God"
is sin. How can any sensible person ever conceive of the possibility
of a soul living with God with a sinful nature? The grace of God is
wonderful. He loved us. He gave His Son for our redemption, and
that Son poured out His lifeblood to atone for our sins. Who could
measure the height or depth, or length or breadth of such love? Will
we not manifest our love by yielding all that we are and have to Him?

*Our blessed Lord, help us to walk in the light of*
*Your love today as the redeemed of You. Amen.*

...........................................................................................................................

...........................................................................................................................

...........................................................................................................................

...........................................................................................................................

# Day 238
## The Lord of Glory

*Which none of the princes of this world knew: for had they known it,*
*they would not have crucified the Lord of glory.*
1 CORINTHIANS 2:8

What a title is this! Behind it are the eternal years which the mind of
man can never penetrate. "The Lord of Glory"—Creator of all things,
in whom is wrapped up all wisdom and power. "Had they known!"
Oh, the pity of it that eyes are closed and hearts bolted against the
revelation of our Lord who descended from the heights of glory and
went into the depths of human sorrow and suffering in order to reveal
Himself to sinful men. Pity the poor princes of this world who resist
the entreaties of the Holy Spirit to receive Him as Savior and Lord.

*Oh gracious Lord, make our meditations of You sweet today. Amen.*

.................................................................................................................

.................................................................................................................

.................................................................................................................

.................................................................................................................

# Day 239
## *The Foundation*

*For other foundation can no man lay than that is laid,*
*which is Jesus Christ.*

1 CORINTHIANS 3:11

Here we have a wonderful title for our Lord—"Jesus Christ, the
Foundation." That foundation was laid before the world was created.
There is no other. On this Foundation is built all the purposes of
God for time and for eternity. On it is being built the church, "a holy
temple," and a "habitation of God through the Spirit." How is this
structure to be built? By the Holy Spirit through His own beloved
disciples who are endued and endowed with power to go into the
world and gather the stones of human souls. What a wonderful work
is assigned to us, working in harmony with Him.

*Dear Lord, be with us today as we seek to gather to Yourself precious*
*souls who will become stones in Your temple. Amen.*

...................................................................................................................................

...................................................................................................................................

...................................................................................................................................

...................................................................................................................................

# Day 240
## Our Passover

*Purge out therefore the old leaven, that ye may be a new lump, as ye are unleavened. For even Christ our passover is sacrificed for us.*
1 CORINTHIANS 5:7

The Jews had their Passover which commemorated their flight from Egypt which God accomplished with a high hand and a stretched-out arm. It was a foretaste of our Passover—a Lamb without blemish, slain for our sins, whose blood sprinkled on our hearts cleanses from sin, and whose broken body feeds our souls. With us it is a *daily* feast. By it we are separated from the worldly Egypt and safe forevermore. Therefore, let us keep the feast with the unleavened bread of sincerity and truth.

*Lord Jesus, in sweet fellowship we would sit at Your feet and feast on You, today. Amen.*

.......................................................................................................................
.......................................................................................................................
.......................................................................................................................
.......................................................................................................................

# Day 244

## *That Spiritual Rock*

*And did all drink the same spiritual drink: for they drank of that spiritual Rock that followed them: and that Rock was Christ.*

1 CORINTHIANS 10:4

Paul is calling attention to the journey of the children of Israel through the wilderness and comparing it to the life of the church. They were supernaturally supplied daily with food and water. The water was a gift from God, symbolizing the Water of Life which springs from the spiritual Rock, which is Christ. He is our Rock, and from His torn side flow rivers of living water. How often we have sung, "Jesus the Water of Life will give, freely, freely, freely"—and then how often we have forgotten to slake our thirst from that Fountain which will never cease to flow down through the ages.

*Lord Jesus, our spiritual Rock, help us to drink freely of Your living water today. Amen.*

.......................................................................................

.......................................................................................

.......................................................................................

.......................................................................................

# Day 242
## *The Head of Every Man*

*But I would have you know, that the head of every man is Christ.*
1 CORINTHIANS 11:3

God reigns supreme in this world, but God is manifested in the flesh in the person of Jesus, who is supreme over all humanity, and every man is morally bound to acknowledge and obey His authority. He is the "head over all things to the church" (Ephesians 1:22). Were the church to acknowledge His authority and become obedient to His command, what a different condition would exist. As Head of the church He has given orders to "Go into all the world and preach the gospel," but His command has not been obeyed. Let us bow to His mandate and let every one of us seek to do our part.

*Lord Jesus, we bow to Your mandate today.*
*Help us to tell the story of the cross to a lost world. Amen.*

..........................................................................................................................

..........................................................................................................................

..........................................................................................................................

..........................................................................................................................

# Day 243

## The Firstfruits of Them That Sleep

*But now is Christ risen from the dead,*
*and become the firstfruits of them that slept.*
1 CORINTHIANS 15:20

Here is an emphatic statement, "Now *is* Christ risen." There can be
no controversy over this fact. The church itself is the challenge to all
doubters. The Bible, the lives of believers, all witness to the fact of
His resurrection. He is the *firstfruits*, and every believer looks forward
with glad anticipation to the coming day of all days when the trumpet
will sound and "the dead in Christ shall rise first" (1 Thessalonians
4:16). This is the blessed hope—to be with Him and like Him forever.

*Make this a glad day, our Lord, as we contemplate this wonderful*
*truth and think of You as the coming, glorious One. Amen.*

.......................................................................................................

.......................................................................................................

.......................................................................................................

.......................................................................................................

# Day 244

## The Last Adam

*And so it is written, The first man Adam was made a living soul;
the last Adam was made a quickening spirit.*

1 CORINTHIANS 15:45

The *first* Adam was created out of the dust of the earth, and God
breathed into his nostrils the breath of life. The *last* Adam was
conceived by the Holy Ghost. He was a "God-Man." The first Adam
was innocent; the last Adam was holy. The first became a sinner; the
second was sinless. He was a life-giving Spirit. He was the Life-giver
and the Light-giver. Through this last Adam, through faith, we receive
the nature which prepares us for an eternal inheritance and qualifies
us for the celestial joys of the celestial city.

*Our Lord, You have quickened us by the indwelling Spirit,
and we meditate with grateful hearts on You, the last Adam. Amen.*

.....................................................................................................................

.....................................................................................................................

.....................................................................................................................

.....................................................................................................................

# Day 245

## *The Lord from Heaven*

*The first man is of the earth, earthy;*
*the second man is the Lord from heaven.*
1 CORINTHIANS 15:47

The contrast here again is between Adam and Christ. Adam was of the earth. The Lord was from heaven. The first man was a failure, and all men are born in sin and are failures. Therefore, the necessity of a "Man from heaven." Our eyes are fixed on Him today—this "Second Man." All men bear the image of the earthy, but to bear the image of the heavenly, Christ should be their desire. Let us seek, by holy fellowship with Him today, to reflect His image in this sinful world.

*Lord Jesus, help us to walk with You today. Amen.*

# Day 246

## A Quickening Spirit

*And so it is written. . .the last Adam was made a quickening spirit.*
1 CORINTHIANS 15:45

We are of the earth, earthy, by birth, but we have a new birth. What was first natural and earthy; afterward comes the spiritual. How wonderful is the operation of God in creating in fallen man an eternal life! "He that hath the Son hath life" (1 John 5:12). These mortal bodies will become, through the power of our Lord as the quickening Spirit, glorious, immortal bodies in which He will dwell throughout the eternal years. What a glorious outlook for us whose eyes are turned heavenward where we look for Him.

*Oh quickening Spirit, come quickly! We long to see You! Amen.*

......................................................................................................

......................................................................................................

......................................................................................................

......................................................................................................

# Day 247
## The Image of God

*In whom the god of this world hath blinded the minds of them which believe not, lest the light of the glorious gospel of Christ, who is the image of God, should shine unto them.*

2 CORINTHIANS 4:4

Satan is the god of this world and the prince of the power of the air. The eyes of every unsaved person have been blinded to the vision of Christ who is the image of God. Their minds are on earthly things in which there is no joy, no peace, no satisfaction. Satan hates our Lord with a bitter hatred, and as the days pass and the coming of the Lord draws near, Satan's blinding powers are more and more manifest. This fact should stir our hearts to increased desire and intensified purpose to present to the unsaved, Jesus, the Image of God, who is so precious to us.

*Lord Jesus, fill us with Your Holy Spirit and give us a passion for the blinded souls of the unsaved. Amen.*

.............................................................................................................................

.............................................................................................................................

.............................................................................................................................

.............................................................................................................................

# Day 248
## The Unspeakable Gift

*Thanks be to God for his unspeakable gift.*
2 CORINTHIANS 9:15 ASV

Paul has been praising the Corinthians for their liberal gifts to
the saints in Judea. His heart is full and he breaks out in a note of
praise as he thinks of God's greater gift of His Son—"Thanks. . .for
his unspeakable gift." There was no treasure which God could give
comparable to the gift of His Son, and "Having given us his Son, will
he not with him freely give us all things?" How could it be possible
that the Father would give to sinners the Son of His Love? How we
ought to love Him! Is there anything we have or are that we would
withhold from Him?

*Loving Lord, help us to sense in a new way what it means for us
to possess You, the unspeakable Gift. Amen.*

# Day 249
## Christ

*Blessed be the God and Father of our Lord Jesus Christ, who hath blessed us with all spiritual blessings in heavenly places in Christ.*
EPHESIANS 4:3

Three times is the word "bless" used in this verse. God is a blessed God, and He showers His blessings on His people. What are the spiritual blessings in Christ? They are spiritual gifts, the blessing of the Gospel—the "Good News" from God. They include the eternal purpose and precious promises of God which are to be manifested in the present, in the future, and throughout eternity. As you read your Bible, note them. How many! How strengthening! How encouraging! How satisfying! How enduring! And all *in* Christ and *only* in Him.

*How we rejoice, oh Christ of God, that by faith we are in You and all of Your blessings are for us. Help us to appropriate them with thankful hearts. Amen.*

........................................................................................................

........................................................................................................

........................................................................................................

........................................................................................................

# Day 250

## *Head over All Things*

*And hath put all things under his feet,*
*and gave him to be the head over all things to the church.*
EPHESIANS 4:22

The gift of God to the church—which is His body—was Christ,
whom He raised from the dead and seated Him above all principalities
and powers and might and dominion and every name which is
named both in this world and in that which is to come. We need to
recognize our exalted position—bone of His bone and flesh of His
flesh—chosen in Him before the world was—dear as the apple of
His eye. Let us live in the enjoyment of our great privileges and in
the assurance that through the endless ages we will be His blessed,
beloved ones.

*Oh Head of the church, keep us in happy, holy, heavenly fellowship*
*with Yourself this day, and until You come! Amen.*

.............................................................................................................................

.............................................................................................................................

.............................................................................................................................

.............................................................................................................................

# Day 254

## *He That Filleth All in All*

*Which is his body, the fulness of him that filleth all in all.*
EPHESIANS 1:23

The church is the "fulness of Christ." Christ could never be complete without the church, and the church could never be complete until the last member is brought into the body. Therefore, the business of the church is to be busy seeking to save the lost. Every soul added increases His fullness. The life of Christ pulses through His Body, the church, and through each individual member. Why, then, are we not filled with Christ? Because we are not yielded to the indwelling Holy Spirit who imparts the life of Christ and who takes the things of Christ and shows them to us.

*Blessed Holy Spirit, give us a passion to know more and more of Him that "filleth all in all." Amen.*

........................................................................................................

........................................................................................................

........................................................................................................

........................................................................................................

# Day 252

## Our Peace

*For he is our peace, who hath made both one,*
*and hath broken down the middle wall of partition between us.*
EPHESIANS 2:14

"He is our Peace." Thank God, we have everything in Him. In the poor, old world, we have tribulations, trials, disappointments, sorrows of all kinds, but there never will be a time when we may not rest our heads on His shoulder and be at peace. Christ has reconciled both Jew and Gentile, and the old wall of separation is broken down. He has reconciled men with God. Remember His words that last night with His disciples: "Peace I leave with you, my peace I give unto you. . . Let not your heart be troubled, neither let it be afraid" (John 14:27).

*Blessed Lord Christ, we look to You with glad hearts*
*and pray that the peace of God that surpasses understanding*
*may garrison our souls today. Amen.*

# Day 253
## One Lord

*One Lord, one faith, one baptism.*
EPHESIANS 4:5

The apostle is stating in this and the succeeding verses a great truth concerning the church. There is a sevenfold unity. One *body*—composed of believers. One *Spirit*—the Holy Spirit who dwells within every believer and unites them together in the common bond. One *hope*—the blessed hope of His coming. One *Lord*—the Lord over all. One *faith*—and that founded on the one Lord. One *baptism*—and that the baptism of the Holy Spirit. One *God and Father* of all—the object of our faith and in whose name all believers are baptized. We are not our own. We were bought with a great price. We are His subjects, under His rule and authority.

*Lord Jesus, let us bow to You as the one Lord*
*and with loyal hearts yield to Your authority. Amen.*

...............................................................................................................................

...............................................................................................................................

...............................................................................................................................

...............................................................................................................................

# Day 254
## The Head

*But speaking the truth in love, may grow up into him in all things,
which is the head, even Christ.*
EPHESIANS 4:15

We have already viewed Christ as the "Head over all things," but here
we have Him as the Head of the body of believers—the church. There
is inspiration in this thought—that we are to grow up into Him. How
are we to do this? We have His life within us. The Head dominates
the body and according to the need, the supply is furnished. The new
nature demands a supply which cannot come from any other source
than the Head. What a wonderful body the church would be, were it
always mindful of its Head and responding to His desire for it!

*Lord, help us to look on You, the great Head of the Church,
and as members of Your body, grow into Your likeness. Amen.*

# Day 255

## An Offering

*And walk in love, as Christ also hath loved us,*
*and hath given himself for us an offering.*
EPHESIANS 5:2

Hear Him speaking that last night, "Greater love hath no man than this, that a man lay down his life for his friends" (John 15:13). What an offering for those disciples who deserted Him that very night! He became sin for us. He said, concerning the offering of His life, "I have power to lay it down, and I have power to take it again" (John 10:18). No man could take His life without His consent, who through the eternal Spirit offered Himself without spot to God.

*Lord Jesus, we recognize Your offering in our behalf.*
*Help us to walk in love as You have also loved us,*
*and may our fellowship with You be sweet today. Amen.*

.......................................................................................................

.......................................................................................................

.......................................................................................................

.......................................................................................................

# Day 256

## A Sacrifice to God

*And walk in love, as Christ also hath loved us,*
*and hath given himself. . .a sacrifice to God.*
EPHESIANS 5:2

God's holiness and righteousness demanded some way by which sin could be forgiven and removed, so that sinful men could have access to Him and live in fellowship with Him. There was only one way. Sin—violation of law—must be punished and the sinner must be justified from all things. The Law of Moses could not do this. The offerings of the Old Testament could not do it. But God had a way. So "now once in the end of the age hath he appeared to put away sin by the sacrifice of himself." "It is finished" were His words on the cross. Through His sacrifice our sins were washed away and rights and titles to heaven granted us.

*Lord, forbid that we should ever hesitate to sacrifice all for You! Amen.*

# Day 257
## A Sweet-Smelling Savor

*And walk in love, as Christ also hath loved us,*
*and hath given himself. . .for a sweetsmelling savour.*
EPHESIANS 5:2

When Noah came out of the ark he took of every clean beast and of every clean fowl and offered a burnt offering to the Lord. "And the LORD smelled a sweet savour" (Genesis 8:24). When Christ laid down His life on the cross what a perfume went up to God—the perfume from the sacrifice of His Son! Has the perfume of the cross yet reached you? It reached heaven. Has the love of God, as manifested in the sacrifice of His Son, mastered you?

*Our Father, forgive us that we have been so unmindful*
*of the wonders of Your love. May its perfume pervade our lives,*
*and through us, the lives of others. Amen.*

# Day 258

## A Servant

*But made himself of no reputation, and took upon him the form of a servant, and was made in the likeness of men.*
PHILIPPIANS 2:7

Isaiah spoke concerning Him: "Behold, my servant shall deal prudently, he shall be exalted and extolled, and be very high" (Isaiah 52:13). "His visage was so marred more than any man" (Isaiah 52:14). The meaning of the word "servant" is "a doer" or "a slave." He was God manifest in the flesh, but "He emptied himself," made Himself of "no reputation." Christ is the second Adam. He is the representative of perfect manhood. As a servant, He humbled Himself. From what lofty heights—Creator of all things down to a servant of men, step-by-step in service to the whipping post and the cross. What an example for us is He—the Servant!

*Oh Christ our Beloved, help us to follow in Your footsteps and be in deed and in truth Your chosen servants. Amen.*

......................................................................................................

......................................................................................................

......................................................................................................

......................................................................................................

# Day 259

## The Lord Jesus Christ

*To the saints and faithful brethren in Christ which are at Colosse:*
*Grace be unto you, and peace, from God our Father*
*and the Lord Jesus Christ.*

COLOSSIANS 1:2

Master! Savior! Anointed! Here, as in many other places in the epistles, we have a combination of names. "Grace and peace from God the Father and the Lord Jesus Christ." They are One. Mystery of mysteries! Hundreds of names and titles are given to Him, but after all, He has said, "I and my Father are one. He that hath seen me hath seen the Father." When he descends from heaven we will see Him in whom all these titles are vested. Grace has its fountain in Him, and always in every emergency and under every condition and circumstance, His grace will be sufficient.

*Gracious Lord Jesus Christ, manifest Your grace unto us today. Amen.*

..................................................................................................................

..................................................................................................................

..................................................................................................................

..................................................................................................................

# Day 260

## His Dear Son

*Who hath delivered us from the power of darkness,*
*and hath translated us into the kingdom of his dear Son.*
COLOSSIANS 1:13

To "his dear Son" is here attributed the deliverance and translation
of the believer from the power of Satan, the ruler of this dark world.
Ignorant of Him, millions are dwelling today, controlled by the
power of a Satanic nature, resisting His Word, and doomed to eternal
darkness. There is only One who can deliver men. It is His dear Son.
We are the possessors of this truth and have experienced it. How can
we, how dare we, be indifferent to the blinded souls all around us
when His dear Son is longing to have them respond to His call "Come
unto Me"?

*Oh beloved Son, make us light-bearers to darkened souls today. Amen.*

.............................................................................................................

.............................................................................................................

.............................................................................................................

.............................................................................................................

# Day 264

## *The Image of the Invisible God*

*Who is the image of the invisible God, the firstborn of every creature.*
COLOSSIANS 1:15

It is difficult for us to refrain from loud acclamation as we view this expression concerning our Lord, the very "Image of the Invisible God!" We look at Him and we see God. We hear His voice and we hear God. We see him holding the children in His arms, and we see God. We see Him in the home of friends, and we see God. We see Him feeding the multitudes, and we see God. There is but *one* God, and He is the One. "Great is the mystery!" Great is our expectation! Glory to God in the highest! We know Him. We love Him. We wait with longing hearts for Him.

*Lord Jesus, in whom dwells all the fullness of the Godhead bodily, we worship You! We adore You! We look and long for You. Amen.*

# Day 262

## *The Firstborn of Every Creature*

*Who is the image of the invisible God, the firstborn of every creature.*
COLOSSIANS 1:15

"The firstborn of every creature," meaning "of every thing made." So many statements in the scripture make plain the fact that God and Christ are One. He is the manifestation of God. He unites man and God. The invisible God has become visible to men in Jesus Christ. He is the Sovereign Lord of creation, by primogeniture the Head of the natural creation and of the new creation, so that He is intimately allied to us. He is the first begotten from the dead. We could write a book about it, but a Book *has* been written.

*Blessed Lord, our Firstborn, to whom we are united forever,*
*help us to glorify You today. Amen.*

........................................................................................................................

........................................................................................................................

........................................................................................................................

........................................................................................................................

# Day 263
## *Creator of All Things*

*For by him were all things created.*
COLOSSIANS 1:16

He is the Creator of *all* things—visible and invisible! Reflect on this for a moment. Do not allow the magnitude of this revelation to escape you as your eyes are resting on your loving Lord. Are we not prone to underestimate Him and undervalue His Work? See how Paul visualizes it in Ephesians 3:8–9: "Unto me, who am less than the least of all saints, is this grace given, that I should preach among the Gentiles the unsearchable riches of Christ; And to make all men see what is the fellowship of the mystery, which from the beginning of the world hath been hid in God, who created all things by Jesus Christ." Should we not take a place lower than Paul who counted himself the least of all saints?

*Lord, help us. Keep ambition and pride from dominating us.*
*Keep us at Your feet in worship and praise. Amen.*

# Day 264

## *The Head of the Body*

*And he is the head of the body, the church: who is the beginning,*
*the firstborn from the dead; that in all things he*
*might have the preeminence.*

COLOSSIANS 1:18

The Word of God emphasizes this fact over and over again, and we
need to have it emphasized so that we can be always viewing Him in the
proper spirit. The church is His Body. We are members of that Body.
We are one with Him. What is involved in this? We must recognize our
relationship and think of Him always as our Head and look to Him for
wisdom and guidance. We must joyfully seek to walk in fellowship with
Him, do His good pleasure, and in all things please Him.

*Lord Jesus, great Head of the church, help us to honor You*
*today by lip and life. Amen.*

.......................................................................................................................

.......................................................................................................................

.......................................................................................................................

.......................................................................................................................

# Day 265

## The Beginning

*Who is the beginning, the firstborn from the dead.*
COLOSSIANS 1:18

He is the Beginning. Who is? The "Firstborn from the dead." By His resurrection, He inaugurated a new era, the beginning of a new life— eternal life. He is the "firstfruits of them that slept" (1 Corinthians 15:20), the Prince of life. He solved the problem forever. He rose from the dead. He conquered death. His resurrection assures the resurrection of the bodies of all those who sleep in Him. The mystery is solved. There can be no end to this eternal life which we have through faith in Him, for it is His life. Let us stop and meditate today on all that it means.

*Blessed Lord, who are the beginning of that life in us that is insured forever, help us to tell the story to others. Amen.*

..............................................................................................................................................

..............................................................................................................................................

..............................................................................................................................................

..............................................................................................................................................

# Day 266

## The Firstborn from the Dead

*And he is. . .the firstborn from the dead;*
*that in all things he might have the preeminence.*
COLOSSIANS 1:18

Here we have the origin of Christ's headship. "{He is} the firstfruits of them that sleep" (1 Corinthians 15:20), or "have fallen asleep." He is the Originator of spiritual life, "The Beginning of the new creation of God." He died and was among the dead. Through death, He paid the penalty for sin and was raised for our justification "from *among* the dead." Others were translated or were raised but died again. He rose to die no more. This resurrection guarantees His headship and insures the resurrection of all believers. He has the preeminence in all things.

*Our Lord Jesus, we glorify Your name as the Firstborn from the*
*Dead and look forward to the day when we also will be raised and,*
*with glorified bodies, abide with You forever. Amen.*

.......................................................................................................

.......................................................................................................

.......................................................................................................

.......................................................................................................

# Day 267
## *Hope of Glory*

*To whom God would make known what is the riches*
*of the glory of this mystery among the Gentiles;*
*which is Christ in you, the hope of glory.*

COLOSSIANS 1:27

Here is a revelation not made known in other ages to the sons of men but now revealed by the Holy Spirit to the church. Paul is continually impressing the wonderful truth of God's will as the cause and work of salvation, and the wonderful privilege bestowed on him of preaching it. This glory which is so wonderful is the garment with which all believers will be clothed when the Christ comes for us. How we should prize the possession of "Christ in us." Do we, and do we long that others might possess it also?

*Lord, give us a hunger for others that they might also be*
*the rich possessors of the Hope of Glory. Amen.*

..........................................................................................................................

..........................................................................................................................

..........................................................................................................................

..........................................................................................................................

# Day 268

## Christ Our Life

*To whom God would make known what is the riches*
*of the glory of this mystery among the Gentiles;*
*which is Christ in you, the hope of glory.*

COLOSSIANS 1:27

Hallelujah! What a promise is this: "When he shall appear!" He will change these bodies of our abasement and fashion them like unto His own glorious body. Our life is in Him, "For to me to live is Christ" (Philippians 1:21). He could not appear without us. He is preparing a place for us. He is coming for us. The anticipation of this is the great incentive of our life. These mortal bodies will be clothed like unto His glorious body. There can be no condition in life here which can rob us of the joy of this great truth. Let us breathe this atmosphere and look forward to that glorious day of our manifestation.

*Our Lord, our Life, we will seek to honor You today*
*and pray that it may be a glad day. Amen.*

.............................................................................................................

.............................................................................................................

.............................................................................................................

.............................................................................................................

# Day 269
## *All and in All*

*Where there is neither Greek nor Jew, circumcision nor*
*uncircumcision, Barbarian, Scythian, bond nor free:*
*but Christ is all, and in all.*

COLOSSIANS 3:44

Christ is the Creator of all things. "Without him was not any thing
made that was made." He is in all things. In Him we live and move
and have our being. He is the beginning and the end of all things. He
is the criterion by which all things must be measured. All power is in
Him. All dominion, all authority is vested in Him. All distinctions
are swept away. There is neither Jew nor Greek, old or young, rich
or poor, learned or ignorant, bond or free. He unifies all by His
indwelling Holy Spirit.

*Lord, help us to recognize this blessed truth, enjoy it,*
*abide in it, and so glorify You today. Amen.*

..................................................................................................................

..................................................................................................................

..................................................................................................................

..................................................................................................................

# Day 270
## The Lord Christ

*Knowing that of the Lord ye shall receive the reward*
*of the inheritance: for ye serve the Lord Christ.*
COLOSSIANS 3:24

We are servants of the Lord Christ. We may never receive what we
think we should or what we hope for in this world, but we are sure
of a proper compensation when God's books are opened, and He
will render to every man according to his deed. Earthly masters will
disappoint us; our heavenly Master—never! No greater privilege
was ever accorded to men than that of serving the Lord Christ. Let
us seek to keep this in mind day by day. We are heirs to a wonderful
inheritance, and our portion will be assigned to us. What a joy to be a
servant to such a Master!

*Lord Christ, may our eyes be on You as we take up*
*the tasks of the day and joyfully serve You. Amen.*

........................................................................................................

........................................................................................................

........................................................................................................

........................................................................................................

# Day 271

## *Lord of Peace*

*Now the Lord of peace himself give you peace always by all means.*
*The Lord be with you all.*

2 Thessalonians 3:16

Our Lord is the Author of peace. He came to make peace possible.
"Peace I leave with you, my peace I give unto you" (John 14:27). In
order to have this wonderful peace we must be yoked close to Him.
We live in a world of unrest and conflict. The heart of humanity beats
high with excitement. "No peace for the wicked!" How we should pity
them. They do not know Him. They can never know Him unless He
is revealed to them. We are His spokesmen. Let us cheerfully make
Him manifest today.

*Lord of Peace, we rest our heads on Your bosom.*
*Your peace surpasses understanding. We thank You. Amen.*

.............................................................................................................

.............................................................................................................

.............................................................................................................

.............................................................................................................

# Day 272

## Our Hope

*Paul, an apostle of Jesus Christ by the commandment of God*
*our Saviour, and Lord Jesus Christ, which is our hope.*

1 TIMOTHY 1:1

He is "our Hope." His promises assure us and fix our faith on Him.
He is the center of the life of a true believer. We could not think of
the coming glory without eyes fixed on Him. The incentive of a loyal
life is to please Him. What could be more satisfying after a day of toil
and burden-bearing than to remember how His Word was our comfort
and His promises our peace? We look at the rising sun as it bathes the
mountain peaks with its glory and at the glittering stars at night, and
they foretell the coming of the glorious day when He will have us with
Himself.

*Lord, our Hope, our faith is fixed on You.*
*Help us to rest on You today. Amen.*

# Day 273
## *Christ Jesus*

*Christ Jesus came into the world to save sinners;*
*of whom I am chief.*
1 TIMOTHY 1:15

"The Anointed Savior" came into the world to save sinners. Where did He come from? He came from the glory. Who was He? He was God, the Creator. "I came forth from the Father, and am come into the world," He says in John 16:28. Sin separates man from God and separates God from man. Sin is opposition to God. Mankind is under the curse of sin and has no power to atone (make a covering) for its sin. God alone could meet the issue and solve the problem, and He has. He came and bore man's sin on the cross and paid the penalty with His own blood.

*We bow in Your presence, Anointed Savior, and pour out our souls*
*with gratitude to You. Help us to live close to You today. Amen.*

.............................................................................................................

.............................................................................................................

.............................................................................................................

.............................................................................................................

# Day 274
## *The Mediator*

*For there is one God, and one mediator between God and men,*
*the man Christ Jesus.*

1 TIMOTHY 2:5

God is One, and there is but *one* Mediator between God and man and that is a Man; but that Man—praise God—is the man Christ Jesus. He is the Mediator of the New Testament, for by means of death for the redemption of men He alone is qualified to act in man's behalf. He loved us. He died for us. Christ is God, but Christ is also the Head of humanity and He alone is capable of filling the position of Mediator. How wonderful He is, and He is all we need.

*Blessed Mediator, our Sin-bearer, we open our hearts to*
*You as we confess our sins and look with satisfaction*
*on the blood of Your atonement. Amen.*

.................................................................................................................................

.................................................................................................................................

.................................................................................................................................

.................................................................................................................................

# Day 275
## *The Man Christ Jesus*

*For there is one God, and one mediator between God and men,*
*the man Christ Jesus.*

1 TIMOTHY 2:5

We have considered Christ as Mediator and now we have the
emphasis on Christ, our Mediator, as the *Man* Christ Jesus. In these
days when He is being demeaned by so many who are robbing Him of
His deity, we should rejoice in the privilege offered us of magnifying
Him as both man and God. "Great is the mystery of godliness: God
was manifest in the flesh" (1 Timothy 3:16). No picture in the Bible
is so marvelously thrilling, so calculated to convince and convert, as
that of God dying for men. Hold Him in your thoughts and see Him
today—arms outstretched above a bloodstained body, saying, "Come
unto me. . .I will give you rest" (Matthew 11:28).

*Oh crucified, risen God-Man, we adore You.*
*Guide us today in our worship and work for You. Amen.*

......................................................................................................................

......................................................................................................................

......................................................................................................................

......................................................................................................................

# Day 276
## God Manifest in the Flesh

*And without controversy great is the mystery of godliness: God was manifest in the flesh, justified in the Spirit, seen of angels, preached unto the Gentiles, believed on in the world, received up into glory.*
1 TIMOTHY 3:16

Here is a sermon of marvelous mystery. In a few words we have given to *us* the magnitude of the mission of Christ in leaving the glory and coming to this earth, clothed in the garments of flesh; accomplishing His divine mission of redemption while in human form; leaving His witnesses to His crucifixion, resurrection, and ascension to His high and holy place in glory. We should stand with uncovered heads and with hearts beating in adoration, worship Him as the Holy Spirit of God emphasizes to us this great truth: He came, He died, He lives in us, and He lives in the glory, and we will dwell forever with Him.

*Holy Spirit, help us to magnify and glorify the God-Man. Amen.*

# Day 277

## *Blessed and Only Potentate*

*Which in his times he shall shew, who is the blessed and only Potentate, the King of kings, and Lord of lords.*
1 TIMOTHY 6:15

This term is used only once in the Bible and means the "All Powerful One." Limitless power is His. It is to be manifested at His appearing who is King of kings and Lord of lords. This will be the final event. Our Lord will reveal Himself and will bring with Him the crowns for the victors who have waged a good warfare and stand ready to receive the promised prize, which none can dispute His authority or right to bestow. Paul is so overcome with this vision that he breaks out in notes of highest acclaim (read the sixteenth verse).

*Oh Mighty One, we unite with Your servant Paul and ascribe honor and power to Your name. Amen.*

.................................................................................................................................

.................................................................................................................................

.................................................................................................................................

.................................................................................................................................

# Day 278

## The Judge of Quick and Dead

*I charge thee therefore before God, and the Lord Jesus Christ,*
*who shall judge the quick and the dead. . . . Preach the Word.*
2 TIMOTHY 4:1-2

The Christian life is a solemnly serious life to live. It is a stewardship, and a day of accounting must come. We must *all* appear before Him to give an account for the deeds done in the body. There is no escape from our responsibility for obedience to the command "Preach (tell) the Word (of God); be instant in season and out of season." How solemn! Every man's work will be tried by fire of what sort it is. Gold, silver, precious stones; wood, hay, stubble! It is for us to decide. No one can change the record—neither God nor man. Are you ready?

*Lord Jesus, we look for Your coming. Help us to do our best*
*today to make Your will and Your way known. Amen.*

.........................................................................................................................

.........................................................................................................................

.........................................................................................................................

.........................................................................................................................

# Day 279

## *The Righteous Judge*

*Henceforth there is laid up for me a crown of righteousness,
which the Lord, the righteous judge, shall give me at that day.*
2 TIMOTHY 4:8

In the judgment spoken of here there is a promised reward which Paul speaks of as coming to himself and to all those who love the truth concerning the coming of the Lord. They are to be crowned, and the Lord will Himself put the crown on the head of those who are true to His promises and look for Him—a "crown of righteousness." There are many crowns awaiting the saints. Salvation is a *gift*, but crowns are for those whose lives have been lived in obedience to the Word of God. His shed blood should be the appeal to us to be willing to lay down our lives for Him.

*Lord Jesus, give us an increasing desire to see You and be with You.
Help us to complete the Body and thus hurry Your coming. Amen.*

..........................................................................................

..........................................................................................

..........................................................................................

..........................................................................................

# Day 280

## *The Great God*

*Looking for that blessed hope, and the glorious appearing*
*of the great God and our Saviour Jesus Christ.*
TITUS 2:13

For whom are we looking? Everywhere it is stated in the scripture that we are to look for our Lord—for Jesus Christ who died. "This same Jesus. . .shall so come. . .as ye have seen him go" (Acts 1:11). He will come with His glorified body; with the hands that were pierced; with the wounded side from which the lifeblood was poured out; with the scarred brow where the thorns left their marks. The same voice that said "Behold my hands and my feet. It is I, be not afraid" will welcome us when we meet Him in the air.

*Lord Jesus, we wait with expectant hearts, and our voices are tuned*
*for the "Hallelujah Chorus" as we say, "Come." Amen.*

.................................................................................................................

.................................................................................................................

.................................................................................................................

.................................................................................................................

# Day 284

## God Our Savior

*But after that the kindness and love of God*
*our Saviour toward man appeared.*
TITUS 3:4

This is not the first time that the title "God our Savior" has been used. We find it in 1 Timothy 1:1, where the reference, no doubt, is to the call of Paul as recorded in Acts 13:2. Here it refers to God as our Savior. Jesus said, "I and my Father are one" (John 10:30) and He is our Savior. When we sing "Savior, More Than Life to Me," we recognize the almighty power and authority of God our Savior. Let us look up to Him today. By our God-given right we have been regenerated and renewed by the Holy Spirit and should exercise our rights as His children.

*Let us open wide the door of our hearts to You, our God and Savior,*
*and give You the right-of-way today. Amen.*

# Day 282

## *Heir of All Things*

*Hath in these last days spoken unto us by his Son, whom he hath appointed heir of all things, by whom also he made the worlds.*
HEBREWS 1:2

How logical the Bible is. To our Lord is ascribed glory because He is the Creator of all things. He made the worlds. He says, "All things that the Father hath are mine" (John 16:15). Unlimited power is His. Unlimited possessions are His. We are also His. Praise God, what a revelation we have of Him! He purchased us with His own precious blood. We are dear to Him as the apple of His eye. He will never leave us nor forsake us. We belong to the "heir of all things." Our needs will be supplied, then, for we are heirs of God and joint-heirs with Jesus Christ. Let us keep our heads erect and our eyes turned heavenward.

*Blessed "heir of all things," take us under Your wings today and may we be gloriously happy in fellowship with You. Amen.*

.................................................................................

.................................................................................

.................................................................................

.................................................................................

# Day 283
## *The Brightness of His Glory*

*Who being the brightness of his glory.*
HEBREWS 1:3

Do you want to visualize the glory of God? Then gaze on Jesus Christ. When we see Him, we see God, for He is God. Oh, the marvel of the Godhead! How wonderful it is! How fascinating is this Bible of ours in which we have such a revelation of God as manifest in the flesh! Moses prayed to God, "I beseech thee, shew me thy glory" and the answer was, "I will make all my goodness pass before thee" (Exodus 33:18–19). With your Bible in hand, meditate on this revelation of Jesus Christ and rejoice in Him as your own Lord.

*Father, let the rays of sunshine from the person*
*of Christ shine in our hearts today. Amen.*

..................................................................................................................

..................................................................................................................

..................................................................................................................

..................................................................................................................

# Day 284

## The Express Image of His Person

*Who being the brightness of his glory,*
*and the express image of his person.*
HEBREWS 1:3

"No man hath seen God at any time, the only begotten Son, which is in the bosom of the Father, he hath declared him" (John 1:18). We have seen the Father for we have seen the Son. We have seen Him, a man among men, eating, drinking, living, working with them. When a seal is stamped on a piece of paper, we have its exact image. When we see Jesus we see the God-Man—a *perfect* representation of God, and we see the *only* God we will ever see. Hold that truth and meditate on it for a while, and let the Holy Spirit magnify Christ to you. Thank God, we have seen Him, we know Him, we love Him, we are one with Him.

*Lord, let us bask in the sunshine of Your love today and mold and fashion us more and more in conformity to Your image. Amen.*

........................................................................................................

........................................................................................................

........................................................................................................

........................................................................................................

# Day 285
## *The Upholder of All Things*

*Who being the brightness of His glory, and the express image of his person, and upholding all things by the word of his power.*
HEBREWS 1:3

God is Light. Jesus is the radiance of that light. God is the Sun, and Jesus is the Sunbeam. The sun and sunshine are coexistent. We see the *sunbeam*, not the sun itself, but the *rays* of the sun. If you break a sunbeam through a prism, you have all the colors. When Jesus was broken on the cross, all of the richness of the glory of God was manifested. He is the express image of the person of God. He is the Upholder of all things. He created all things. He purged all sin. In the hollow of His hand are all things. You can trust all to Him.

*Lord Jesus, we thank You for Your finished work. We rest in You. Keep us trustful and faithful until Your coming. Amen.*

........................................................................................................................

........................................................................................................................

........................................................................................................................

........................................................................................................................

# Day 286

## *The Sin Purger*

*Who. . .when he had by himself purged our sins,*
*sat down on the right hand of the Majesty on high.*
HEBREWS 1:3

How lightly we think of sin. It is so common that we fail to view it
in God's light. "Coming short of the glory of God" is sin. Sin has
never changed because human nature has never changed. Every child
born into this world is born with the Adam and Eve nature. There is
no exception. One sin makes a sinner and shuts the door to heaven.
Christ came as the Sin-purger and opened the door to heaven. We only
need to tell our fellowmen the story and point them to the open door.
"I am the Door," He says. "By me, if any man enter in, he shall be
saved" (John 10:9). God help us to tell hungry-hearted men the story.

*Oh Sin-purger, we give to You all the praise and ask for tender*
*hearts in telling the story to sinful men. Amen.*

# Day 287

## God

*But unto the Son he saith, Thy throne, O God, is for ever and ever.*
HEBREWS 1:8

Here we have the alpine height in titles for our Lord, "Thy throne, O *God*!" All other names are inferior to this. When He was born in a manger, God was there. When He worked at the carpenter's trade, God was there at work. When He associated with the fishermen, it was God who was their companion. When He spoke, God spoke. When He died on the cross, it was God Himself who poured out His life. When He comes "with a shout," it will be the voice of God that calls us to be with Him forever. It is God the Son who holds the scepter and rules the worlds, and we will rule and reign with Him.

*Oh God our Savior and Coming King, hurry Your coming and help us to help You hurry that day, for Your own name's sake. Amen.*

....................................................................................................................

....................................................................................................................

....................................................................................................................

....................................................................................................................

# Day 288

## *The Captain of Our Salvation*

*For it became him. . .to make the captain of their*
*salvation perfect through sufferings.*
HEBREWS 2:10

We cannot do anything but bow our heads as we read this verse and meditate on the Captain of our salvation and His perfection. He was God and He was Man, we have learned. As Man He must be manifest in the life. He is the Son of God, the Captain (or "Author") of salvation. We are the *sons* of God. The mode and method of perfection is manifested by our Leader. He was tempted; so are we. He suffered; so must we. He was persecuted; so must we be. He paid the price; so must we. The climax for Him and for us is glory.

*Let us bow our heads and hearts to our Leader today and obey His orders. He will be with us in every trial and suffering. Amen.*

# Day 289
## The Seed of Abraham

*For verily he took not on him the nature of angels;*
*but he took on him the seed of Abraham.*
HEBREWS 2:16

This suggestive title surely draws a picture well worthy of our consideration. Why did He not take on Himself the nature of angels? Do not the fallen angels need help? Are they inferior to men? Will they evolve into good angels? No, but those angels who fell did so in full consciousness of all that it meant. He came to fallen man and took on Himself the "seed of Abraham" because He longed to lift us to heights above those ever known to angels.

*Our Lord, the wonder of Your work for us astonishes us.*
*Keep us, we pray, from being selfish. Help us to tell the story*
*of Your love to our fellow men. Amen.*

.............................................................................................................................

.............................................................................................................................

.............................................................................................................................

.............................................................................................................................

# Day 290
## *The Apostle*

*Consider the Apostle and High Priest of our profession,
Christ Jesus.*

HEBREWS 3:1

Jesus was an Apostle (or "Sent One"). He was sent with the Gospel (Good News). God sent prophets and angels to bear His messages to men. He sent Moses, the mighty man of God. But now we are looking at the Apostle from heaven's court itself. He came to bring the most wonderful message ever intended for mortal ears: "God so loved the world!" Why did He so love it, and how was that love manifested? This Apostle did His work and has appointed us, who are believers, to carry it on to fallen men. This Apostle was faithful. Are we? We are His authorized representatives.

*Help us to be Your "sent ones" today, bearing the joyful message of salvation to those who do not know it. Amen.*

# Day 294
## *The High Priest*

*Consider. . .the High Priest of our profession, Christ Jesus.*
HEBREWS 3:1

We are called to consider Jesus Christ as High Priest. We are called "holy brethren." We cannot be called on too often to consider Him as our High Priest seeing that "he ever liveth to make intercession for {us}" (Hebrews 7:25). Could we only make it our life habit to, every morning, spend a few moments in contemplation of Him as *our* High Priest and take up life's duties with that picture before us, seeing Him clothed in the garments of the High Priest, in the Holy of Holies, we would be better believers.

*May our eyes be on You today, great High Priest. Amen.*

.............................................................................................................................

.............................................................................................................................

.............................................................................................................................

.............................................................................................................................

# Day 292
## *The Builder*

*For this man was counted worthy of more glory than Moses,*
*inasmuch as he who hath builded the house hath more*
*honour than the house.*

HEBREWS 3:3

Christ is here identified as "the Builder" or "Establisher" of the
house. He is the Apostle. He is the High Priest. The foundation
of the house is laid in Him. "Ye are God's building," Paul says in
1 Corinthians 3:9. We are temples of the Holy Spirit now. Christ
dwells within us. We are to be built up into a holy temple from which
will go out the voices of millions of the redeemed as they sing the
"Hallelujah Chorus." Let Christ have His way in fitting us for our
appointed places in the Temple of God, for He is the Master Builder
and we are to share with Him in the coming day.

*Grant to us, Lord, submission to Your Holy*
*will in all things this day. Amen.*

# Day 293
## *The Great High Priest*

*Seeing then that we have a great high priest, that is passed into the heavens, Jesus the Son of God, let us hold fast our profession.*
HEBREWS 4:14

Jesus, the Son of God, is our great High Priest. Where is He? In the glory, at the right hand of the glory of God. What is He there for? To represent us. He carried the blood offering with Him and presented it in the Holy of Holies. He has seated Himself. He is our representative. We can come with boldness to the throne of grace and will find grace for every need. He is the Son of God with power. Let us hold fast our confession. He loves us. He took our place on the cross. He settled every claim against us. Satan may condemn us, but our great High Priest holds out His pierced hands and that is enough.

*Lord Jesus, while You are representing us in the glory beyond, help us to represent You here. Amen.*

........................................................................................

........................................................................................

........................................................................................

........................................................................................

# Day 294
## A Priest Forever

*Thou art a priest for ever after the order of Melchisedec.*
HEBREWS 5:6

He is our High Priest, our Great High Priest, and He is also a Priest forever after the similitude of Melchisedec (Genesis 14:18–20), that strange character who typified our Lord. Will Christ be our representative throughout eternity? Yes—and *we* will be *His* representatives throughout eternity. For our new life is eternal. Our habitation will be eternal. How it warms our hearts to think of that word "forever" in connection with our relation to Christ! He is our eternal High Priest, and we are to be kings and priests in association with Him (Revelation 1:6). We are poor, undone, hell-deserving sinners, but through Him, we are lifted to eternal heights.

*Lord, great High Priest, help us to honor You by lip and life. Amen.*

.............................................................................................

.............................................................................................

.............................................................................................

.............................................................................................

# Day 295

## Author of Eternal Salvation

*And being made perfect, he became the author of*
*eternal salvation unto all them that obey him.*

HEBREWS 5:9

Christ was perfected through suffering. He was obedient unto death, even the death of the cross, and through the hard, cruel, sacrificial journey, which He made to the cross—suffering beyond the power of thought to comprehend—He perfected a way by which men could be saved. When He bore our sin on the cross, the unchanging law of God was in operation, and He suffered separation from God. There was only one way by which sinful men could be made righteous, and that was by the Savior's taking our place, which He did, and now His obedient followers share with Him the glory.

*In every time of testing, sorrow, or suffering, may we look to You,*
*our eternal salvation, and find the promised comfort and help. Amen.*

# Day 296
## The Forerunner

*Whither the forerunner is for us entered, even Jesus.*
HEBREWS 6:20

"Our hope is fixed on nothing less than Jesus' blood and righteousness." Our hope is an anchor, entering into that which is beyond the veil, and our Forerunner has entered beyond the veil into the Holy of Holies. Our hope is anchored in Him. How safe it is! How satisfying it is! We are a part of Him. We can never be separated from Him because He lives in us, and we will live and be with Him forever. Let our souls go out in unbounded thanksgiving.

*Lord Jesus, our great Forerunner, we rejoice in You today. You are in the glory. We are looking forward to being with You and like You. Come quickly and receive us to Yourself. Amen.*

........................................................................................................

........................................................................................................

........................................................................................................

........................................................................................................

# Day 297
## *King of Righteousness*

*First being by interpretation King of righteousness.*
HEBREWS 7:2

The picture is taken from the story of Melchisedec, the strange king to whom Abram paid tithes (Genesis 14). Christ is King of righteousness, for He is the King of kings. He is *the* Righteous One and the *only* Righteous One. We have no righteousness. All of our righteousness is like filthy rags, but "Christ is the end of the law for righteousness to every one that believeth" (Romans 10:4). We believe in Him, and it is counted to us for righteousness. His righteousness is put to our account, and we are associated with the Righteous King forever. Hallelujah!

*Lord, we confess our unworthiness, but we rejoice in Your finished work and in the gift of Your righteousness to us. Amen.*

.............................................................................................................................

.............................................................................................................................

.............................................................................................................................

.............................................................................................................................

# Day 298
## King of Peace

*After that also King of Salem, which is, King of peace.*
HEBREWS 7:2

Righteousness is the basis of peace. There is no peace for the wicked. "He is our peace, who hath made both one, and hath broken down the middle wall of partition between us. . .for to make in himself of twain one new man, so making peace" (Ephesians 2:14–15). Remember what the King of Peace said, "Peace I leave with you, my peace I give unto you. . . Let not your heart be troubled, neither let it be afraid" (John 14:27). He dwells in us, and we dwell in Him. He came and preached peace. He went to the cross and made peace possible. "Great peace have they which love thy law" (Psalm 119:165).

*Oh King of Peace, may Your peace which surpasses all understanding garrison our souls today. Amen.*

# Day 299
## *The Surety*

*By so much was Jesus made a surety of a better testament.*
HEBREWS 7:22

Sometimes we lack assurance. We tremble, perhaps, and lack
confidence in the finished work, which our Christ has accomplished
for us. But we have here the statement that Christ has become our
Surety, or Security. We are made confident by the fact that He has
placed Himself as our Bondsman, our Security. We can draw our
drafts on the Bank of heaven, and He has pledged Himself as our
Security. "Whatsoever ye shall ask in my name, that will I do" (John
14:13). Why have we so little faith in His pledged Word? Giving does
not impoverish Him, nor withholding enrich Him.

*Let us honor Him by asking today, in His precious Name,*
*large things for His glory. Amen.*

.......................................................................................................................

.......................................................................................................................

.......................................................................................................................

.......................................................................................................................

# Day 300

## *Our Intercessor*

*Wherefore he is able also to save them to the uttermost that come unto*
*God by him, seeing he ever liveth to make intercession for them.*
HEBREWS 7:25

He saves to the fullest extent for He forever lives and He forever
represents us and meets all the charges against us. "And he saw that
there was no man, and wondered that there was no intercessor:
therefore his arm brought salvation unto him; and his righteousness,
it sustained him" (Isaiah 59:16). The Holy Spirit also makes
intercession for us with "groanings which cannot be uttered" (Romans
8:26). Satan may bring charges against us, and sometimes they may be
well founded, but He is there. He bore our sins, carried our sorrows,
meets every accusation. What a wonderful Savior and Intercessor!

*Our Lord, we draw near in full assurance of faith.*
*You will never leave us nor forsake us. We glorify Your*
*name now and will forever throughout eternity. Amen.*

.............................................................................................................................

.............................................................................................................................

.............................................................................................................................

.............................................................................................................................

# Day 304
## *Separate from Sinners*

*For such an high priest became us, who is. . .separate from sinners.*
HEBREWS 7:26

We use this as a title (or attribute) of our Lord because preachers and teachers are drifting so far away from the belief in the Virgin Birth of our Lord, denying that He was God manifest in the flesh and lining up with the Unitarian belief. But remember the sin question could only be settled by a *sinless* Man—a *spotless* Lamb. Such was He who *knew* no sin though He *became* sin for us that we might become the righteousness of God in Him. But, though He was separate from sinners, He did not avoid them as we are likely to do. No one ever loved them as He did—the Holy One. We must not miss this suggestion if we are to be like Him, loving sinners and following His example.

*Lord Jesus, give us a real love for lost souls*
*and a passion for their salvation. Amen.*

..................................................................................................................

..................................................................................................................

..................................................................................................................

..................................................................................................................

# Day 302
## *Higher Than the Heavens*

*For such an high priest became us, who is. . .higher than the heavens.*
HEBREWS 7:26

This wonderful High Priest, the spotless Lamb of God, when He had finished His priestly sin offering, sat down at the right hand of God. Yet we can see Him, the unchangeable Christ, with wounded hands and feet bearing testimony to His individuality and unchanging personality. Someday from the dizzy heights He will descend with a shout. His voice will ring out in glad expectancy. He is coming for you and for me. Wonder of wonders! Our faith in His finished work has sealed us forever to Himself.

> *Lord, exalted One, we give You all praise and*
> *wait with glad hearts for Your coming. Amen.*

# Day 303
## The Minister of the Sanctuary

*A minister of the sanctuary, and of the true tabernacle,*
*which the Lord pitched, and not man.*
HEBREWS 8:2

We are carried back to the picture of the Tabernacle and of the Temple
where God's High Priest officiated. He represented God in all of
the ceremonies of the Holy Assembly. Here we have the promised
Messiah, the Lord Jesus Christ, in the capacity of the Minister (or
servant) of the Sanctuary. He is the King, but He is still a Servant of
men, serving in our behalf, loving us, ministering to us. Dwelling in
our heart by the Holy Spirit, He performs every needed function in
the cleansing and preparing of His people for their access to God.

*We thank You, Lord Jesus, for Your*
*marvelous ministry in our behalf.*

.......................................................................................................................................

.......................................................................................................................................

.......................................................................................................................................

.......................................................................................................................................

# Day 304
## Mediator of a Better Covenant

*But now. . .he is the mediator of a better covenant.*
HEBREWS 8:6

We have viewed our Lord as "the Minister of the Sanctuary," and
He is now termed the "Mediator of a Better Covenant." Aaron was
the high priest of the sanctuary of the old covenant, but now Christ
in heaven is the Mediator of a heavenly covenant—God's agreement
to confer blessings on men. He promises to put His laws into their
minds and write them on their hearts and says, "I will be their God
and they shall be my people; their sins and iniquities will I remember
no more." Let us remember, then, that we are His sanctuary, His
temple, and He will perfect His work in and through us. Give way to
His will and let our temples be holy to the Lord.

*Help us, great Mediator, to surrender all to You. Cleanse us and
keep us cleansed that we may offer acceptable worship to You. Amen.*

.......................................................................................................
.......................................................................................................
.......................................................................................................
.......................................................................................................

# Day 305
## *The Testator*

*For where a testament is, there must also of necessity
be the death of the testator.*
HEBREWS 9:16

A testator is a man who makes and leaves a will, or testament, at
death. Christ has left a testament and a will. He died for us. He shed
His blood as a freewill offering in our behalf. Under the law we were
condemned to death. "The soul that sinneth, it shall die" (Ezekiel
18:20). "Death passed upon all men, for that all have sinned"
(Romans 5:12). The sin question is settled forever for us who believe
in Jesus Christ, our Testator. He forever lives. He represents us in the
presence of the Father.

*Lord, we lift our hearts to You and rejoice in the finished
work and testimony of our Testator. Amen.*

# Day 306
## *He That Shall Come*

*For yet a little while, and he that shall come will come,*
*and will not tarry.*
HEBREWS 10:37

The Christian life is built not only on the present but on the unseen future. Our life is a life of faith, a faith tried and tested and proven; fixed on the unerring, unbreakable Word of God. God has never broken a promise, and He never can. We can bank with unfailing confidence on His written and living Word. Nothing pleases our Lord more than implicit faith in His Word and work. Nothing gives us such rest and joy as does this childlike faith. We must not be moved by the theories or doubts of men. When in doubt, read Hebrews 11.

*Lord, we are looking for Your coming in the clouds of glory.*
*Come quickly! Amen.*

# Day 307
## A Rewarder

*But without faith it is impossible to please him:*
*for he that cometh to God must believe that he is,*
*and that he is a rewarder of them that diligently seek him.*
HEBREWS 11:6

We come to God only through Jesus Christ, "No man cometh unto
the Father, but by me" (John 14:6). And our Lord Jesus Christ is
the Judge (John 5:22). "For the Father judgeth no man, but hath
committed all judgment unto the Son." He pronounces the sentence.
He gives the reward (Revelation 22:12). "And, behold, I come quickly;
and my reward is with me." What we do we must do in His name and
for His Glory (Colossians 3:24), "Knowing that of the Lord ye shall
receive the reward of the inheritance: for ye serve the Lord Christ."
We must live for Him and be willing to die for Him. Our reward
awaits us.

*Lord, we commit ourselves to You.*
*Use us this day for Your glory. Amen.*

......................................................................................................................

......................................................................................................................

......................................................................................................................

......................................................................................................................

# Day 308
## The Finisher of Faith

*Looking unto Jesus the. . .finisher of our faith.*
HEBREWS 12:2

He is the Captain and leads His hosts with the Sword of the Spirit in His hand. And He is the Finisher (Completer) of our faith. Our Lord set us the example of faith, and He will perfect it in us. We see Jesus who, for the joy that was set before Him, endured the cross, despised the shame, and is now set down at the right hand of God. He *finished* His work of faith, and by grace He will finish it in our experience. There will be trials, there will be severe testings, but we are to "count it all joy." He did, and day by day and step-by-step, He leads us on. The best is always before us, though the last link may be the cross— but then, "Face-to-face with him!"

*Lord, hold us fast by the power of faith until we finish our course. Amen.*

.......................................................................................................................

.......................................................................................................................

.......................................................................................................................

.......................................................................................................................

# Day 309
## *The Author of Faith*

*Looking unto Jesus the author. . .of our faith.*
HEBREWS 12:2

The Author (Leader) of our faith is Jesus. Look to Him, for the inspiration to faith is found in Him. He is the prophesied and promised "Seed of the woman," bruised by Satan. He paid the penalty and then robbed the grave of its power, rose in the majesty of His glorified body, and will come someday to bruise the serpent's head, master, and imprison him. He inspires us by His sacrificial death and by His precious promises. His message is "Follow me. I will never leave thee nor forsake thee." And our response to Him should be, "Lead on; we will follow Thee even unto death."

*Oh great Author of our Faith, keep our eyes on You, and with unwavering faith may we follow You to the end. Amen.*

.......................................................................................................................

.......................................................................................................................

.......................................................................................................................

.......................................................................................................................

# Day 310
## Mediator of the New Covenant

*And to Jesus the mediator of the new covenant, and to the blood
of sprinkling, that speaketh better things than that of Abel.*
HEBREWS 12:24

The Christian life is a strange life, a journey through wilderness
experiences, but we always have something better before us. The
doorposts are sprinkled with blood. We are safe. Old things have
passed away. The blood of Jesus Christ, God's Son, cleanses us from
*all* sin. The blood speaks of His sacrificial, finished work. Let our
eyes rest on the cross. Let us see the blood. Let us rest under it. Let
it separate us from a sinful world and make of us witnesses to its
cleansing power, and let us magnify its efficacy to a sin-sick world.

*Lord, give us the needed grace to witness today and every day to
the efficacy of the atoning blood of the New Covenant. Amen.*

.............................................................................................................................

.............................................................................................................................

.............................................................................................................................

.............................................................................................................................

# Day 344
## *My Helper*

*So that we may boldly say, The Lord is my helper.*
HEBREWS 43:6

What a difference there is in believers! How timid some are. Is it because they do not know the promises? "The fear of man bringeth a snare: but whoso putteth his trust in the LORD shall be safe" (Proverbs 29:25). "The angel of the LORD encampeth round about them that fear him, and delivereth them" (Psalm 34:7). Courage of conviction is the crying need of the Christian today—conviction based on God's Holy Word and God's call to service. He has said, "I will never leave thee, nor forsake thee" (Hebrews 43:5). Faith takes hold on this promise and allows nothing to move it.

*Lord Jesus, our Helper, help us to lean hard on Your gracious promises and have a joyful life today. Amen.*

....................................................................................................

....................................................................................................

....................................................................................................

....................................................................................................

# Day 312
## Jesus Christ the Same

*Jesus Christ the same yesterday, and to day, and for ever.*
HEBREWS 13:8

"The same!" How we love this verse. The world is a sinful, restless world. Uncertainty is written everywhere in human life, but the Living Word and the written Word are unchangeable. What was He before He was born of the Virgin Mary? He was God. What was He when He lived and labored among men? He was God. What was He when He hung on the cross? He was God. What is He today? Still God, with the same pierced hands and feet, the same scarred side, the same loving heart—for having loved His own, He loves them still and will love them throughout eternity. Nothing in human thought or language is more wonderful.

*Lord Jesus Christ, You are the same. Help us to sense it and intensify our love for You and may it also be always "the same." Amen.*

.................................................................................................................

.................................................................................................................

.................................................................................................................

.................................................................................................................

# Day 343

## The Great Shepherd of the Sheep

*Our Lord Jesus, that great shepherd of the sheep.*
HEBREWS 13:20

In the sixth chapter of Mark we have a touching picture of our Lord Jesus. He had been apart with His disciples in a desert place, and "when he. . .saw much people, {he} was moved with compassion toward them, because they were as sheep not having a shepherd: and he began to teach them many things" (Mark 6:34). He was the promised Shepherd. He is here pictured as the Great Shepherd, raised from the dead, sanctified by the blood of the everlasting covenant, which is able to make us "perfect in every good work to do his will" (verse 21). How? By working in us and through us what pleases Himself.

*Lord, we are Your sheep. Take us, mold us, and make of us what will please You, and we will give You all the glory. Amen.*

# Day 314
## *That Worthy Name*

*Do not they blaspheme that worthy name by the which ye are called?*
JAMES 2:7

James is dealing here with the theme of prayer. He urges the saints not to have the faith with respect to persons and gives them a needed lesson on partiality in our attitude toward men because of their wealth or position. The emphasis is on "The Worthy Name." That Name is sacred, "for there is none other name. . .whereby we must be saved" (Acts 4:12). God has "given him a name which is above every name: that at the name of Jesus every knee should bow" (Philippians 2:9–10), though for some who are compelled to bow, it will be too late. In that Name we approach our Father; in that Name we have our title to the glory land.

*Lord Jesus, we come in Your Worthy Name and ask for forgiveness for our sins of neglect and ask for Your power for service today. Amen.*

..................................................................................................................

..................................................................................................................

..................................................................................................................

..................................................................................................................

# Day 315
## A Lamb without Blemish or Spot

*But with the precious blood of Christ,*
*as of a lamb without blemish and without spot.*
1 PETER 1:19

Our familiarity with scriptural terms often causes us to minimize
their meaning. Here we have two words so marvelously wonderful
that we are hesitant in our effort to make any comment—"Blood"
and "Lamb." How precious the Blood! Millions and millions of
drops were poured out through the ages from Abel to Christ and every
one of them said: "The Lamb is not yet. But He will come. We are
the testimony of His coming." And finally the spotless, pure Lamb
of God finished the work of redemption. Is He precious to us? So
precious that we would be willing to die in His behalf? If so, let us say
to Him,

*Oh Lamb of God, my Savior, purchased by Your precious blood,*
*I surrender all to You now. Amen.*

........................................................................................................................

........................................................................................................................

........................................................................................................................

........................................................................................................................

# Day 346
## A Chief Cornerstone

*Behold, I lay in Sion a chief corner stone. . .*
*and he that believeth on him shall not be confounded.*
1 PETER 2:6

Every structure must have a foundation, and those of special honor must have a cornerstone. Christ is the Chief Cornerstone of the most wonderful temple ever conceived. This temple is built of human lives—blood-washed saints of the Living God. It is the dwelling place of God the Father, God the Son, and God the Holy Spirit. Over the doors are inscribed the words, "Holiness unto the Lord." From the dome the chimes ring out the call, "Exalt the LORD our God, and worship at His holy hill" (Psalm 99:9).

*Oh Lord, may we be the mouthpieces to spread the invitation*
*to others to come to the temple for worship. Amen.*

.................................................................................................................

.................................................................................................................

.................................................................................................................

.................................................................................................................

# Day 317
## A Living Stone

*To whom coming, as unto a living stone, disallowed indeed of men,
but chosen of God, and precious.*
1 PETER 2:4

Words are inadequate to describe the mysteries of heaven. It is not
composed of an inert mass like the stones of earth, but of *living, life-
imparting* stones. He is living. He will always be living. He lives in the
lives of the redeemed. He is the chosen of God. He is the Stone cut
out of the mountain, which is to crush the nations. He is the One in
whom and through whom we have everlasting life. He lives and will
live through eternity, and we will live in and with Him. Hallelujah!

*Dear Lord, our Rock, our Foundation Stone, we rest in the security
of Your eternal life. Manifest that life through us today. Amen.*

.......................................................................................................................

.......................................................................................................................

.......................................................................................................................

.......................................................................................................................

# Day 348
## An Elect Stone

*Behold, I lay in Sion a chief corner stone, elect. . . .*
1 PETER 2:6

The Elect Stone (the "Chosen of God") is the Chief Cornerstone of the Temple of God, which is composed of believers who were chosen before the foundation of the world. Nothing ever occurs by chance with God. He saw this Temple before He created the universe. We were chosen in Him, our Lord, and He was chosen in the council chamber of heaven to become the Elect Stone—the One who should be the Head of the Corner. His plans are all working out for the culminating scene when the gathering will take place at His coming.

*When the time comes, Lord Jesus, may we be among those*
*who will bring our sheaves with us. Amen.*

..............................................................................................................................

..............................................................................................................................

..............................................................................................................................

..............................................................................................................................

# Day 349

## *A Precious Stone*

*Behold, I lay in Sion a chief corner stone. . .precious. . . .*
1 PETER 2:6

How precious He is! The more we know about Him the more wonderful He becomes, and the more intimately we know Him the more precious He is. "To whom coming, as unto a living stone, disallowed indeed of men, but chosen of God, and *precious*" (1 Peter 2:4, emphasis added). Not precious to the world, for the world has no place, no use for Him; but "unto you. . .which believe he is precious" (1 Peter 2:7). He is the Creator. He holds the world in the hollow of His hand as a dry leaf and could crush it. But He so loved you and me that He laid aside His royal robe, arrayed Himself in human flesh, and then poured out His precious blood for us. Should He not be precious to us?

*Lord, we desire in our hearts to hold You precious.*
*Holy Spirit, help us. Amen.*

.......................................................................................................

.......................................................................................................

.......................................................................................................

.......................................................................................................

# Day 320
## A Stone of Stumbling

*The stone which the builders disallowed. . .*
*is made. . .a stone of stumbling.*
4 PETER 2:7–8

A Cornerstone on which the whole world was built, on which the church is built, and a "Stone of Stumbling!" How can that be? To those who willfully reject Him, as did the Jewish nation, and stumble into the abyss, there is weeping and wailing and gnashing of teeth. To those who pride themselves on their education, wealth, or position, and refuse to bow at His feet, He is a Stone of Stumbling. How subtle is Satan! How hard is the human heart! How our hearts ache for those who do not know Him.

*Our Lord, You are precious to us. Help us to remove the stumbling*
*blocks by living out a life that will win some souls to You. Amen.*

......................................................................................................................................

......................................................................................................................................

......................................................................................................................................

......................................................................................................................................

# Day 324

## A Rock of Offense

*The stone which the builders disallowed. . .*
*is made. . .a rock of offence.*
1 PETER 2:7–8

The Jewish nation is an illustration of our theme. Every possible effort was made by Christ to win His own people to Himself. But they would not have Him. What a blow has fallen on them! Driven from pillar to post, peeled, robbed, persecuted, killed, their desire has been granted. "His blood be on us, and on our children" (Matthew 27:25). How will it be in the future? See Revelation 6:15–16. How can it be that our loving, crucified Lord should become to so many a "Rock of Offense" instead of the "Chief Cornerstone?"

*Our Lord, keep our feet on the Rock and our hearts loving You. Amen.*

.............................................................................................................................

.............................................................................................................................

.............................................................................................................................

.............................................................................................................................

# Day 322
## The Bishop of Souls

*For ye were as sheep going astray; but are now returned unto the Shepherd and Bishop of your souls.*
1 PETER 2:25

The elders of the early church were "overseers"—called to care for the flock as undershepherds. Here Christ is set before us as the One who directs the undershepherds. He is "The Bishop." He is the imparter of life, which is eternal, which He purchased for us by His own sacrifice. His eye is on us. He is the One whose heart goes out in love to the lost, straying sheep and who never fails in His own good way and time to bring them back to the fold (the true church). God help those who selfishly seek and faithlessly serve as undershepherds. "Seekest thou great things for thyself? seek them not" (Jeremiah 45:5).

*Lord, help us to recognize You as our Bishop and be subject to Your guidance. Hold us. Keep us. Feed us. Amen.*

# Day 323
## *The Just*

*For Christ also hath once suffered for sins, the just for the unjust.*
1 PETER 3:18

How strong is the contrast here—the *Just* for the *unjust*! Why this sacrifice? That He might bring us to God, making it possible for us to have access through the torn veil to the Holy of Holies. He was the *Just*, the *Sinless One*. "He became obedient unto death" bearing our sins that He might "bring us to God." Sin demands punishment. Jesus kept the law and took our place who were violators of law, setting us free from the penalty and according to us the rights and titles of "just ones." Think of the cross, the agony, the pain, the shameful death—*all* for you and me!

*Oh Just One, You who have paid the penalty and the price for our sins, help us to hold You in our hearts today. Amen.*

.................................................................................................................................

.................................................................................................................................

.................................................................................................................................

.................................................................................................................................

# Day 324
## The Chief Shepherd

*And when the chief Shepherd shall appear,*
*ye shall receive a crown of glory that fadeth not away.*
1 PETER 5:4

Christ as our Shepherd has already been considered as the "Door of the Sheep," "The Good Shepherd," "The One Shepherd," "The Great Shepherd," and now we have the climax in "The Chief Shepherd." In Him is vested all authority and power. He will give the rewards to the faithful. His glory is to be shared by us. Our faithfulness to Him here is to be rewarded there. We visualize Him with shepherd staff leading, guiding, directing His sheep, and enfolding them in safety. But there is the glad day, which is to come, when He will crown His loyal ones. Is there anything more to be desired than the privilege accorded us of making Him now the chiefest of ten thousand in our hearts?

*Lord, be to us today the Altogether Lovely One. Amen.*

# Day 325
## *The Day Star*

*We have also a more sure word of prophecy; whereunto ye do well*
*that ye take heed. . .until. . .the day star arise in your hearts.*
2 PETER 1:19

In the Gospel of John, we read: "In him was life; and the life was
the light of men" (John 1:4). We have the sure Word of God. It is a
lamp to our feet and a light unto our path. Our hearts are darkened by
the evil nature within us, but when Jesus comes into our hearts He
illumines the Word of God and shines with all the effulgence of His
glory. Perpetual day is for those who walk in His light. Every day is a
good day and the eternal glory awaits us.

*Blessed Lord, our Light, shine in our hearts and*
*lives today and may we reflect Your glory. Amen.*

...........................................................................................................................

...........................................................................................................................

...........................................................................................................................

...........................................................................................................................

# Day 326
## Lord and Savior Jesus Christ

*But grow in grace, and in the knowledge of our Lord and Saviour Jesus Christ.*

2 PETER 3:18

"Grow in grace!" Thank God, it is possible and it is our duty so to do. "And in the knowledge of—!" Here we pause and face a most remarkable exhortation. The vastness of the suggestion of growing in the "knowledge of the Lord, the Saviour, Jesus, and Christ" sets before us a task which will last throughout eternity. Growing into Him—this marvelous One whom we do not know, thank God—is a part of eternal life. How will we obey this command? Study His Word. It is the Lamp and Light. Search this Word. It is a mine of treasures. Submit to the commandments of the Word. Then will we be wise indeed.

*Our Lord and Savior, Jesus Christ, bowing in Your glorious presence, we submit to You. Help us to know and love You more and more as the days go by. Amen.*

# Day 327
## The Word of Life

*That which was. . .our hands have handled, of the Word of life.*
1 JOHN 1:1

John 1:1–2 says: "In the beginning was the Word, and the Word was with God, and the Word was God. The same was in the beginning with God," and this truth bewilders us; but here we have John saying concerning Him who was God that he had looked on Him and handled Him. He, Himself, said to doubting Thomas, "Handle me, and see; for a spirit hath not flesh and bones, as ye see me have" (Luke 24:39). He is the Life-giving Word. The need of a lost world is to know Him. The business of believers is to tell the wonderful story. Paint the picture. Live the life. Sow the seed. And you will find Him growing into your own life.

*"God the Word," how we thank You for the revelation of Yourself to us. We are Yours. You are ours. Amen.*

# Day 328
## That Eternal Life

*That eternal life, which was with the Father,*
*and was manifested unto us.*

1 JOHN 1:2

John says, "We have seen Him who is Life Eternal. We are witnesses
to that fact and we want you to have the assurance that your joy
may be full." And Paul says, "For in him dwelleth all the fulness
of the Godhead bodily" (Colossians 2:9). *He is* Eternal Life. He
has imparted eternal life to us through the channel of faith and the
indwelling Holy Spirit certifies to it. Nothing can ever separate us
from the love of God which is in Christ Jesus our Lord. We are God's
rich sons. Our treasures are for evermore. "Oh, happy day, that fixed
our choice!"

*Let us go out and tell it anywhere and everywhere. Oh Blessed One,*
*our Eternal Life, we wait for Your coming. Come quickly. Amen.*

.....................................................................................................................

.....................................................................................................................

.....................................................................................................................

.....................................................................................................................

# Day 329
## *The Advocate*

*My little children, these things write I unto you, that ye sin not.*
*And if any man sin, we have an advocate with the Father,*
*Jesus Christ the righteous.*

1 JOHN 2:1

Sin is the existing nature of man. God, in love, has recognized the need of man and has made provision for that need. We sin when we "come short of the glory of God." So Christ becomes our Advocate or "One who comes alongside," which is the meaning of *advocate*. He comes to stand by us. When Satan charges us with sin, Christ represents us and defends us. He is the Attorney who handles our case. His propitiation (or covering for sin) is manifested in all His work for us—in His life, His death, His resurrection, His ascension, and His intercession.

*Lord, we thank You that You appear for us and, through You,*
*we are all accepted by our heavenly Father. Amen.*

.................................................................................................

.................................................................................................

.................................................................................................

.................................................................................................

# Day 330
## *Jesus Christ the Righteous*

*If any man sin, we have an advocate with the Father,*
*Jesus Christ the righteous.*
1 JOHN 2:1

Jesus Christ is the Righteous One. *Righteous* means "right" or "just."
There never was another perfectly righteous man, for the scripture
says, "There is none righteous, no, not one" (Romans 3:10). "All have
sinned." No unrighteous man could be our Advocate or Judge. He
must Himself be just, and He is, and He is also the Justifier (Romans
3:20). What a consolation to us as poor sinners to know that we are
justified from all things from which we could not be justified by the
Law of Moses.

*Lord Jesus, we pour out our hearts to You. You have settled forever*
*what we could never have settled. Hallelujah! Amen.*

# Day 334

## *The Propitiation*

*And he is the propitiation for our sins: and not for ours only,
but also for the sins of the whole world.*

1 JOHN 2:2

The sin question is the great question. Sin separates us from God.
His wrath against sin must be appeased, satisfied, and the provision
for that satisfaction is in His Son (Romans 3:25): "Whom God hath
set forth to be a propitiation through faith in his blood. . .through the
forbearance of God." Wonderful love of God the Father; wonderful
love of Jesus, His Son our Savior; wonderful love of the Holy Spirit,
the One who makes the fact of propitiation clear to us through the
Word! How is the "whole world" to know this truth? Someone must
go. Will *we* go?

*Oh Loving Lord, Your love is wonderful. The price You have paid is
wonderful. Help us today to tell the wonderful story. Amen.*

......................................................................................................................

......................................................................................................................

......................................................................................................................

......................................................................................................................

# Day 332
## *The Son*

*And we have seen and do testify that the Father
sent the Son to be the Saviour of the world.*

1 JOHN 4:14

The apostle John is making full proof of his ministry. He is testifying
to the truth from his own personal experience, conscious that he is
indwelt by the Spirit and has the new nature. He says that the Son
was sent for one specific purpose—to be the Savior of men, lost men.
The business of the believer is to testify to that fact. The greatest
business in the world is to follow in the footsteps of men like John,
the fisher of men. It is not a question of church membership or of
worldly possessions, but of knowledge of Him. Have you seen Him?
Do you know Him? Then go and testify of Him.

*Son of God, Savior of lost men, send us out
with Your love message today. Amen.*

.................................................................................................

.................................................................................................

.................................................................................................

.................................................................................................

# Day 333
## *The Savior of the World*

*And we have seen and do testify that the Father
sent the Son to be the Saviour of the world.*
1 JOHN 4:14

A lost and ruined world, bound by the shackles of sin, dominated by the demon Satan, helpless and hopeless! What can be done? Only God, the Sovereign against whom the world has sinned, can solve the question, and He has. He sent His Son. We have seen Him by faith and testify to the truth that He is indeed a Savior. He has saved us through faith in His name and finished work. We *must* testify. We *must* bear witness. Wherever we go, whatever we do, let us tell it—"He is a world Savior."

*Lord, may we be faithful witnesses to Your saving
power and tell the love story to all. Amen.*

.................................................................................................................

.................................................................................................................

.................................................................................................................

.................................................................................................................

# Day 334
## The True God

*And we know that the Son of God is come, and hath given
us an understanding, that we may know him that is true,
and we are in him that is true, even in his Son Jesus Christ.
This is the true God, and eternal life.*

1 JOHN 5:20

In His prayer on that last night, Jesus said to the Father: "As thou
hast given him power over all flesh, that he should give eternal life
to as many as thou hast given him. And this is life eternal, that they
might know thee the only true God, and Jesus Christ, whom thou
hast sent" (John 17:2–3). Here it is made evident that "we are in him
that is true, even his Son Jesus Christ, the true God and eternal life."
There is but *one* God. "Great is the mystery of godliness," but we
praise God—*the True God*—that we are in Him and He in us. Nothing
can ever separate us.

*Lord Jesus, You who are the True God, help us to live out that
great and glorious life that You have imparted to us. Amen.*

# Day 335
## *Eternal Life*

*This is the true God, and eternal life.*
1 JOHN 5:20

Jesus is "the True God," and He is "Eternal Life" also. Human life is eternal, for it must be lived here or in another world. It must be spent in the heart of God our Savior or in the abode of Satan. "Where will you spend eternity?" is one of the most solemn questions ever asked of men. The only answer is found in God's Word, and it is answered there a hundred times and in a hundred ways. To believers, eternity means life with God our Savior, and we look forward with joyful anticipation; but to the unsaved, it is a fearful prospect.

*Lord, help us in dealing with people to be truthful and loving as we paint the pictures of a future without a Savior. Amen.*

.............................................................................................

.............................................................................................

.............................................................................................

.............................................................................................

# Day 336
## The Son of the Father

*Grace be with you, mercy, and peace, from God the Father, and from the Lord Jesus Christ, the Son of the Father, in truth and love.*
2 JOHN 1:3

Here is a threefold blessing bestowed by John: "Grace, mercy, and peace from the Son of the Father." This is the testimony of the Father: "This is my beloved Son, in whom I am well pleased" (Matthew 17:5), and He is the *only begotten* of the Father. There is no separation between Father and Son. There is a union which is unspeakable. "He that hath seen me hath seen the Father" (John 14:9). "I and my Father are one" (John 10:30). The blessing is to be bestowed in "truth and love." Truth without love may be cold, hard, harsh. Love without truth may be purely sentimental, but, when combined, they truly represent the message of "the Son of the Father," for the Son *is* the Truth, manifested in Love.

*We pray, our Father, that this benediction of grace, mercy, and peace may rest on us today as we meditate on "the Son of the Father." Amen.*

# Day 337
## *Jesus Christ*

*Grace be unto you, and peace, from him which is, and which was, and which is to come; and from the seven Spirits which are before his throne; and from Jesus Christ, who is the faithful witness, and the first begotten of the dead, and the prince of the kings of the earth.*

REVELATION 1:4–5

Here is a fourfold adoration of our Lord. Four titles are given to Him, the first of which is "Jesus Christ" (the Anointed Savior). "How sweet the name of Jesus sounds to a believer's ear." He is, He was, and He is to come! That completes the vision of Himself. The "seven spirits before the throne" represent the sevenfold operation of the Lord throughout the earth. We must join with the heavenly host and sing his praises.

*Oh anointed Savior, help us to unite with all the heavenly host in glorifying Your name. Amen.*

..................................................................................................

..................................................................................................

..................................................................................................

..................................................................................................

# Day 338
## The Faithful Witness

*Jesus Christ, who is the faithful witness.*
REVELATION 1:5

This was the testimony of Christ Himself when He stood before Pilate (John 18:37): "To this end was I born, and for this cause came I into the world, that I should bear witness unto the truth. Every one that is of the truth heareth my voice." This was His mission—to bear faithful witness. This is the obligation of every believer, "Ye shall be witnesses unto me" (Acts 1:8). This is the failure in a large measure of the church. The unsaved are waiting for the testimony by lip and life of professing Christians, and as they see it, they are convicted by the Holy Spirit.

*May the Holy Spirit Himself so control our lives that we will count it our highest privilege to manifest Him before a gainsaying world. Amen.*

........................................................................................................................

........................................................................................................................

........................................................................................................................

........................................................................................................................

# Day 339
## *The First Begotten of the Dead*

*Jesus Christ, who is. . .the first begotten of the dead.*
REVELATION 4:5

Jesus Christ raised Lazarus from the dead, but He Himself came out from the grave by His own power. Lazarus died again, but Jesus Christ "ever liveth to make intercession for {us}" (Hebrews 7:25). He was the firstborn of the dead. He is the forerunner of the saints who will also be raised from the dead. "But now is Christ risen from the dead, and become the firstfruits of them that slept" (1 Corinthians 15:20). "We know that, when he shall appear, we shall be like him; for we shall see him as he is" (1 John 3:2). "Who shall change our vile body, that it may be fashioned like unto his glorious body" (Philippians 3:24).

*Our Lord, we look and long for Your coming in Your glorified body that we may be with You and like You. Amen.*

......................................................................................................................

......................................................................................................................

......................................................................................................................

......................................................................................................................

# Day 340
## The Prince of Kings of the Earth

*Jesus Christ, who is the. . .prince of the kings of the earth.*
REVELATION 4:5

A glorious title! Sometime in the future there will be a gathering of all the hosts that have ever lived on this earth, and of the hosts of heaven, and in their presence will stand *One* who will be proclaimed "Prince of the kings of the earth—King of kings and Lord of lords!" The kingdoms of the world are His by right and title, and before Him all must bow. He is Lord of all who exercise authority and King of all who reign. He has not yet asserted His authoritative rights. They are still in abeyance, but the day is coming when every scepter will be broken and every crown laid at His feet.

*We praise You, Lord of Hosts, our Savior; we will be with You then. Help us to do our best to hurry the glad day. Amen.*

.............................................................................................

.............................................................................................

.............................................................................................

.............................................................................................

# Day 341

## *The Alpha and Omega*

*I am Alpha and Omega, the beginning and the ending, saith the Lord, which is, and which was, and which is to come, the Almighty.*
REVELATION 1:8

*Alpha* is the first letter of the Greek alphabet, and *Omega* is the last. So our Lord is First and Last. He is the Source of all things. He is the Source of all truth, of all the promises given in the Word of God, of all the prophecies, of all commands, and of all penalties. How great is our Lord, "which is and which was and which is to come"—the All-inclusive One! Everything is involved in the two words "beginning" and "ending," and one word includes it all—"Is."

*Oh Jehovah-Elohim, First and Last, who sees and knows all things, hold us by Your hand. Amen.*

.......................................................................................................................................

.......................................................................................................................................

.......................................................................................................................................

.......................................................................................................................................

# Day 342
## The Almighty

*I am. . .the Almighty.*
REVELATION 4:8

Our Lord Jesus Christ is the All-sufficient One. Listen to His voice—the "I Am" speaking to us. His voice and message demand attention and obedience. We can trust Him and trust His message. Nothing can fail of all that He says. The Bible is an infallible book. Its message is an infallible message, and it says: "I will receive you. And will be a Father unto you, and ye shall be my sons and daughters, saith the Lord Almighty" (2 Corinthians 6:17–18). And again, "He that dwelleth in the secret place of the most High shall abide under the shadow of the Almighty" (Psalm 91:1). What an abiding place for us who are His dear children!

*Oh Almighty One, we submit to You today, and to Your all-power. Help us to dwell with and in You. Amen.*

................................................................................................................

................................................................................................................

................................................................................................................

................................................................................................................

# Day 343
## The First and the Last

*And he laid his right hand upon me, saying unto me, Fear not;*
*I am the first and the last.*
REVELATION 1:17

He was the First-begotten. He said of Himself, "Before Abraham
was, I am" (John 8:58). And John the Baptist said, "He was before
me" (John 1:15). "In the beginning was the Word, and the Word was
with God, and the Word was God. The same was in the beginning
with God" (John 1:1–2). He puts His right hand on us, that hand
of power, and says in tenderest tones, "Fear not." He draws us to
Himself with that same hand and says, "Rest your head on My
shoulder. Have no fear. You are Mine. I purchased you at a great
price. Perfect love casts out fear." He was *First* in His love for us
when we were in sin. He is the *Last One* to forget or forsake us.

*Blessed Lord, may we have that perfect love which casts*
*out all fear. Amen.*

........................................................................................................................

........................................................................................................................

........................................................................................................................

........................................................................................................................

# Day 344

## He That Liveth

*I am he that liveth, and was dead; and, behold,*
*I am alive for evermore, Amen.*
### REVELATION 1:18

He lives and abides forever. He forever lives to make intercession for us. In love for us and through grace He died for us. He bowed His head and gave up His Spirit. The bars of death were broken. He tore them away. He is living now and will live to the ages of ages, and He holds the keys of death and hell (or Hades). "He has the keys"—the complete mastery. He has the right to open and shut. Binding and loosing are at His command. The sting of death is sin and the strength of sin is the law, but thanks be to God who gives us the victory through our Lord Jesus Christ! Praise be to Your name, Victor over death!

*We await Your coming and the shout from heaven. Amen.*

.................................................................................................

.................................................................................................

.................................................................................................

.................................................................................................

# Day 345
## The Morning Star

*And I will give him the morning star.*
REVELATION 2:28

He will give us Himself, for He is the Morning Star. Again, we hear the voice of the Holy Spirit coming with a heart message for the beloved of the Lord. We are bone of His bone and flesh of His flesh. The stars are for the night, and it is night now for this poor old world that lies in the lap of the devil. It grows darker and darker and midnight is upon us, but our eyes are heavenward. We hear His promise. As the "Sun of Righteousness" to Israel He brought them blessings; but before the glad day for Israel comes, the Morning Star must shine, and a ray of light will appear for His own heavenly ones.

*Lord, keep us close to Yourself. Keep us loyal. Keep our eyes on the skies as we labor for You and for Your coming. Amen.*

.........................................................................................................................................

.........................................................................................................................................

.........................................................................................................................................

.........................................................................................................................................

# Day 346
## *The Hidden Manna*

*To him that overcometh will I give to eat of the hidden manna.*
REVELATION 2:17

What is this Hidden Manna? Is it not Himself who is the Bread of Life? The voice of the Holy Spirit is heard speaking to the churches a message for the overcomers. Food awaits them. For twelve thousand and five hundred days manna was rained down from heaven for the children of Israel. From the glory land our Lord feeds His flock with the Word of God—the Word made flesh. We who feed on Him will live forever. We have the white stone and the new name.

*You are speaking to us, our Lord. We hear. We await the day and the new name which You will give to us. Amen.*

.......................................................................................................................

.......................................................................................................................

.......................................................................................................................

.......................................................................................................................

# Day 347
## The Amen

*These things saith the Amen.*
REVELATION 3:14

*Amen* is "So be it" or "So it is." The "Amen" here is our Lord—the Faithful Witness. He has said "Amen" to every truth of the scripture, but the church has failed to follow in His footsteps. She has the truth for she has Him, and He is the Way, the Truth, and the Life, as we have seen; but she has not said "Amen." She says, "I am rich, and increased with goods, and have need of nothing" (Revelation 3:17). She has not been a faithful and true witness. She has been neither cold nor hot but a lukewarm product. God pity her! To what extent are we responsible? God forgive us. God help us.

*Lord, open our eyes to see, our ears to hear and our hearts to believe.*
*Baptize us with the power of the Holy Spirit. Amen.*

.......................................................................................................

.......................................................................................................

.......................................................................................................

.......................................................................................................

# Day 348
## The Faithful and True Witness

*These things saith the. . .faithful and true witness.*
REVELATION 3:14

We have viewed Him as the Faithful Witness, but He is also the Faithful and *True* Witness. Is it not wonderful? How marvelously the Holy Spirit emphasizes the character of Christ for us. Here we have the "Amen" amplified. The word *faithful* asserts the truthfulness of "True," for it implies "real and complete." He had seen what He attested, and He was competent and willing to faithfully witness. Has the church been a faithful and true witness? No, she has not. Let us come a little closer. Have *we* been faithful and true witnesses? Alas, we must bow our heads with shame as we remember our failure. Will we be?

*Oh Lord our Savior, forgive us for our faithlessness as witnesses. Anoint us to stand before a lost world and be* true *at any cost. Amen.*

.............................................................................................................

.............................................................................................................

.............................................................................................................

.............................................................................................................

# Day 349

## The Beginning of the Creation of God

*These things saith. . .the beginning of the creation of God.*
REVELATION 3:14

There are four headships ascribed to our Lord Jesus Christ. First—of the body: "Head over all things to the church, which is his body" (Ephesians 1:22–23). Second—of the race: "Ye are all one in Christ Jesus" (Galatians 3:28). Third—of the creation: "Who is the image of the invisible God, the firstborn of every creature" (Colossians 1:15). Fourth—of every man: "But I would have you know, that the head of every man is Christ" (1 Corinthians 11:3). Let us seek earnestly to recognize the might and power and authority of our Lord who left heaven and laid down His life for us.

*Oh Mighty One, Creator of all things, help us to recognize
You today and to love and serve You. Amen.*

.......................................................................................................................................

.......................................................................................................................................

.......................................................................................................................................

.......................................................................................................................................

# Day 350
## *The Lion of the Tribe of Judah*

*Behold, the Lion of the tribe of Judah. . .hath prevailed to open the*
*book, and to loose the seven seals thereof.*
REVELATION 5:5

The dying prophecy of Jacob was fulfilled in Jesus: "The sceptre shall
not depart from Judah, nor a lawgiver from between his feet, until
Shiloh come" (Genesis 49:10). Judah had no conception that nearly
three thousand years would pass before his prophecy would or could
be fulfilled, or that its fulfillment would involve the glorified Son of
God. The characteristics of a lion are manifest in the life and work
of the Messiah. He will arrest every opposing force of Satan and
establish His universal kingdom. Glory be to God that we will be with
Him and like Him in the final overthrow of Satan's kingdom.

*Lord, help us to be like You now. Help us to wear the armor*
*of warriors and carry the Sword of the Spirit. Amen.*

....................................................................................................

....................................................................................................

....................................................................................................

....................................................................................................

# Day 354
## *The Root of David*

*Weep not: behold, the Lion of the tribe of Judah,*
*the Root of David, hath prevailed.*
REVELATION 5:5

King David was the representative of *royalty*; Moses of the *Law*;
Abraham of the *promises*. Here, Christ is seen in relation to His
throne and kingdom rights. "A Root" from the stem, or branch of
David (Isaiah 11:1). "And there shall come forth a rod out of the stem
of Jesse, and a Branch shall grow out of his roots." Jesus was the
Root that was to rise and reign over the Gentiles and in Him would
the Gentiles trust. He was worthy to open the book because He was
slain. What wonders confront us concerning Him!

*Lord, we marvel more and more that You could ever love us*
*and die for us, You who are the Mighty One. But we bow*
*at Your feet in worship and praise. Amen.*

.............................................................................................................

.............................................................................................................

.............................................................................................................

.............................................................................................................

# Day 352
## *Holy and True*

*How long, O Lord, holy and true, dost thou not judge
and avenge our blood on them that dwell on the earth?*
REVELATION 6:10

This is the heart cry of those who suffered death for Jesus' sake
because they were true to Him in life and testimony. Is it not such a
cry as sometimes bursts out from our own souls as we see the hellish
hatred of Satan for the souls of men? "How long, O Lord, how long,
Thou Holy and True One?" But we must abide in faith. He says,
"What I do thou knowest not now; but thou shalt know hereafter"
(John 13:7). How marvelous is the grace and patience of God our
Savior! But the day is coming when the Righteous Judge will render
His judgment.

*Holy and True One, we look to You in full assurance of faith.
Keep us close to Yourself today. Amen.*

.......................................................................................................

.......................................................................................................

.......................................................................................................

.......................................................................................................

# Day 353
## *The Lamb in the Midst of the Throne*

*For the Lamb which is in the midst of the throne shall feed them,*
*and shall lead them unto living fountains of waters:*
*and God shall wipe away all tears from their eyes.*
REVELATION 7:17

Here is a wonderful picture of our future dwelling place. We are
before the throne of God. Our robes have been made white in the
blood of the Lamb. We will not know hunger or thirst any more. He
that sits on the throne will dwell among us. No more hunger or thirst
for us. He, Himself, will feed us and we will drink from the living
fountains. Tears will be wiped away forever. What has made all this
possible? *One Thing*—the blood! *One Person*—the Lamb! We will
dwell through eternity with Him, be with Him and like Him.

*Wonderful Lord and wonderful Love, help us to dwell forever in*
*Your presence and feed us with the heavenly manna now. Amen.*

........................................................................................................

........................................................................................................

........................................................................................................

........................................................................................................

# Day 354
## The Lamb Slain

*And all that dwell upon the earth shall worship him,*
*whose names are not written in the book of life of the*
*Lamb slain from the foundation of the world.*

REVELATION 13:8

Jesus was ordained from the foundation of the world to suffer on
the cross for our sins. The death of Christ has been efficacious to
put away sin, from the beginning. The only means of salvation for
men has been the shedding of His blood. That was foreknown and
foreordained of God. What a place in our hearts should the Lamb of
God have! What a place should the blood of Christ have, by which
we are redeemed! For "without shedding of blood is no remission"
(Hebrews 9:22).

*Blessed Lamb of God, we adore You. We praise Your name.*
*We rejoice that we are washed in Your blood. Amen.*

.......................................................................................................

.......................................................................................................

.......................................................................................................

.......................................................................................................

# Day 355
## King of Saints

*Just and true are thy ways, thou King of saints.*
REVELATION 15:3

This title is better rendered "King of Nations" or "King of the Ages." What a picture is here! We are standing by the glassy sea, mingled with fire. A judgment is awaiting the nations. Seven angels with the seven last plagues are there. Mark seems to describe this time: "For in those days shall be affliction, such as was not from the beginning of the creation which God created unto this time, neither shall be" (Mark 13:19). But there are the harps of God and the song of Moses. The song is of victory over the beast and his image. What a day! What joy for our adored Lord!

*We want to pledge to You, today, our loyal devotion,*
*King of Nations. Help us to do Your Holy Will*
*until the coming of "the day." Amen.*

........................................................................................................

........................................................................................................

........................................................................................................

........................................................................................................

# Day 356
## Lord of Lords

*For he is Lord of lords, and King of kings:*
*and they that are with him are called, and chosen, and faithful.*
REVELATION 17:14

From the story of the Garden of Eden until the scene described in this verse, the powers of earth and hell have fought against our Lord. The prince of this world and the prince of the power of the air has shown his satanic hatred for Christ, who is the Promised One and who will bruise his head. The world has been the sphere of the conflict of the ages, but, thanks be to God, there is coming a day when that war will cease and that is the day which is portrayed in this verse. All of the kings must bow to Him. It has been an age-long conflict, but the end must come. We look forward to the victory which is prophesied.

*You, who hold the worlds in the hollow of Your hand,*
*hurry the glad, victorious day of Your coming. Amen.*

# Day 357
## King of Kings

*The Lamb shall overcome them: for he is. . .King of kings.*
REVELATION 17:14

He has on His garments and on His thigh the name "King of kings." Who has? The One who was born in a manger and who fellowshipped with fishermen as He longs to fellowship with us today. A sharp sword issues from His mouth—the Sword of the Spirit, which is the Word of God. As His enemies fell before His presence in the Garden, so fall they then. The power of God's Word is *irresistible*. How foolish are they whose feeble hands are raised up against the King of kings—the Mighty One! What judgment awaits all those who oppose Him and His unerring Word.

*King of kings, we bow to You. We follow You.*
*Help us to fight the good fight of faith. Amen.*

...................................................................................................................

...................................................................................................................

...................................................................................................................

...................................................................................................................

# Day 358
## Lord God Omnipotent

*And I heard as it were the voice of a great multitude, and as the voice of many waters, and as the voice of mighty thunderings, saying, Alleluia: for the Lord God omnipotent reigneth.*
REVELATION 19:6

Here is a climax. What words can compare with the words of God which are associated with this matchless scene: "And after these things I heard a great voice of much people in heaven, saying, Alleluia; Salvation, and glory, and honour, and power, unto the Lord our God. . . . Let us be glad and rejoice, and give honour to him: for the marriage of the Lamb is come, and his wife hath made herself ready" (Revelation 19:1, 7). The time is not far distant. He is coming, the Omnipotent One—and we will be with Him. Alleluia!

*Oh Mighty One, brace us with Your strength that we may do our best to hurry that glad day. Amen.*

.......................................................................................................

.......................................................................................................

.......................................................................................................

.......................................................................................................

# Day 359
## *Faithful and True*

*And he that sat upon him was called Faithful and True.*
REVELATION 19:11

To no one else could that title be applied but the Lord Jesus, who was Himself the Way, the Truth, and the Life. He was faithful to the truth always and faithful in its application, whether in promises of blessings or cursing. Listen to the precious promise, "I will come again, and receive you unto myself; that where I am, there ye may be also" (John 14:3). But the other is equally true, "Depart from me, all ye workers of iniquity. There shall be weeping and gnashing of teeth" (Luke 13:27–28). There is no change in Him, the Living Word, and not one jot or tittle can be changed in the Written Word.

*Lord, we believe in You and in Your Word. May we never depart from it. Keep us faithful and true to You until the long-expected call comes and we will be taken up to be with You forever. Amen.*

........................................................................................................................

........................................................................................................................

........................................................................................................................

........................................................................................................................

# Day 360
## *Word of God*

*And he was clothed with a vesture dipped in blood:
and his name is called The Word of God.*
REVELATION 19:13

How can we attempt to embody in a few words what this title
demands? John only uses the term. John says, "without him was not
any thing made that was made. . . . And the Word was made flesh"
(John 1:3, 14). How glad we are that we have heard His Word. We
have seen Him by faith. He dwells in us and among us. Clothed in a
blood-dipped vesture, He leads the armies of heaven, including all the
saints of the Old and New Testament, to victory. Pity those whose
eyes have been closed to the vision of the real Christ and who only
have a sentimental conception of Him.

*We bow at Your feet, blessed Word of God, and lift our voices
as we sing, "Hallelujah! What a Savior!" Amen.*

....................................................................................................

....................................................................................................

....................................................................................................

....................................................................................................

# Day 364

## The Temple

*And I saw no temple therein: for the Lord God Almighty*
*and the Lamb are the temple of it.*

REVELATION 24:22

What a wonderful Temple! He is the Temple! The city is foursquare,
as was the Holy of Holies; twelve thousand furlongs—fifteen
hundred square miles! Whatever significance there may be in the
dimensions and the structure—whether literal or pictorial—it means,
"Great in size; rich in adornment." The city is of pure gold, like clear
glass; walls of jasper, upon that sapphire, then chalcedony, emerald,
sardonyx, sardius, beryl, topaz, chrysoprasus, jacinth, amethyst;
gates of one pearl; streets of gold. We stand in awe, but—glory be to
God—we anticipate with increasing joy the vision which awaits us and
its full realization.

*Blessed One, keep us close to You with open ears and open eyes,*
*as we await the realization of our fond anticipation. Amen.*

.................................................................................

.................................................................................

.................................................................................

.................................................................................

# Day 362
## The Light of the City

*And the Lamb is the light thereof.*
REVELATION 21:23

The Lamb is the "Light of the World" and He is also the Light of the Eternal, Foursquare City. There is no need of sun or moon, for He who created all things has provided a Light for the City and it is the glory of His own countenance—the Lamb of God who died on the cross; the One who bore our sins and washed us in His own blood. By this Light the nations will walk, and in this Light kings and people will pay their tribute. We will be there. Hallelujah!

*Lamb of God, Light of the World, we bask in the sunshine of Your love now and will in the light of Your glory hereafter. Amen.*

.............................................................................................

.............................................................................................

.............................................................................................

.............................................................................................

# Day 363
## *The Offspring of David*

*I am the root and the offspring of David,
and the bright and morning star.*
REVELATION 22:16

Christ is the Stem, which sprang from the root of Jesse, and He is the Offspring of David. God, the Son, created the heavens and the earth and all that are therein, yet He is the Offspring of David, David's Lord, and David's Son. He was *born* King of the Jews and *died* King of the Jews and some day He will *reign* King of the Jews. This was God's promise, and all of God's promises will be fulfilled. As the Divine Creator, He is the Root of David's house; as Man, He is the Offspring. He sends His angel to give this testimony to us and to the world. There is no contradiction in God's Word concerning God's Son.

*We glorify Your Word and Your work, our Lord.
We look into Your face and adore You. Amen.*

.......................................................................................................................

.......................................................................................................................

.......................................................................................................................

.......................................................................................................................

# Day 364
## The Bright and Morning Star

*I Jesus have sent mine angel to testify unto you these things
in the churches. I am. . .the bright and morning star.*
REVELATION 22:16

We have meditated on Christ as the "Day Star" and the "Morning Star," but here He, who is the Light of the World, speaks of Himself as the "Bright and Morning Star." Before the rising of the sun, before the millennium dawns, He will be to the church the "Bright and Morning Star." He will dispel the darkness for us before the prophesied judgments come upon a weary, sin-sick world; and before the glories depicted in this chapter are revealed, He will appear as the Bright and Morning Star. We must never cease to cherish this great truth, keeping our eyes fixed and our hopes centered on Him.

*Lord, we are looking for the effulgent glory of Your presence,
Bright and Morning Star. Amen.*

# Day 365
## *The Testifier*

*He which testifieth these things saith,*
*Surely I come quickly. Amen. Even so, come, Lord Jesus.*
REVELATION 22:20

This is not a title, nor a name, but a fitting truth with which to close this little volume. We would rejoice if every reader has a heartfelt desire to say "Amen" to this promise of our Lord. The days grow darker for the church and for the world. The signs multiply as we look carefully at the prophecies. The poor old world reels like a drunken man to its doom. Our hearts are sad. We are thinking of those whose future is to be full of woe and anguish. "The Testifier" entreats us to go and testify to the lost. Let us point them to the Lamb of God and plead with sinners to accept Him and with the saints to look for Him. He has left *the Testimony*. And now, in closing, the last verse of this chapter is our heartfelt prayer for our readers:

*"The grace of our Lord Jesus Christ be with you all."* Amen.

.......................................................................................................................
.......................................................................................................................
.......................................................................................................................
.......................................................................................................................

# Index of Names

# Scripture Index